MORE NEEDLEPLAY

BOOKS BY ERICA WILSON

More Needleplay

Ask Erica

Plastic Canvas

Animal Kingdom

Say It with Stitches

*The Craft of Silk and Gold Thread
    Embroidery and Stumpwork*

Needleplay

The Craft of Blackwork and Whitework

The Craft of Crewel Embroidery

Erica Wilson's Embroidery Book

Fun with Crewel Embroidery

Crewel Embroidery

MORE NEEDLEPLAY

ERICA WILSON

CHARLES SCRIBNER'S SONS / NEW YORK

This book is dedicated to needlewomen everywhere.

Library of Congress Cataloging in Publication Data

Wilson, Erica.
  More needleplay.

  1. Embroidery. I. Title.
TT770.W56   746.4′4   79-702
ISBN 0-684-16073-0

FRONTIS: Erica with Margaret McLeod, her producer, in action at WGBH studios in Boston.

ACKNOWLEDGMENTS

My special thanks to photographers Seth Joel, Yale Joel, Leonard Nones, Beverly Hall, Jack Shipley, Paul Frankian, and my husband Vladimir Kagan. My thanks also to *Family Circle* Magazine for the photos of pansies on page 55 and roses on page 90.

Photograph of the Summer Palace, page 26, from *Imperial Peking* by Lin Yutang, copyright © 1961 by Elek Ltd., reproduced by permission of Crown Publishers, New York; illustrations on pages 77, 79, 170 and 172 by special permission of Frederick Warne and Company, from Beatrix Potter's *The Tale of Peter Rabbit, Cecily Parsley's Nursery Rhymes,* and *The Story of a Fierce Bad Rabbit.*

CONTENTS

INTRODUCTION

MAKING a TV series for PBS was a memorable experience. When Rick Hauser first came to Nantucket to talk about it, I thought it would be a vague possibility some six months afterward. Not at all. Two weeks later I found myself in Boston making a pilot!

"I see you are always late and always in a hurry," Rick said. So he had a set built that looked like my living room. I would wait for a signal, dash through the door, trailing wools, frames, and the latest project, breathlessly apologize for being late, show my latest inspirations, and, at the sound of a clock chiming in the distance, rush out again. Well, the set never looked exactly like my living room. I couldn't actually say, "Sorry I'm late," because the recorded show would be aired at the same time each week by the PBS stations. I never heard the delicate chiming of a clock, so a loud gong had to be substituted. But I certainly *was* breathless—with fright! I would stand behind the door waiting for "5 4 3 2 1—run" and my heart would be beating so hard I could hardly hear the countdown. Once, as I was doing a program about men's ties, just before I had to burst through the door, all smiles, I heard a cameraman mutter, "Glad she's not my wife, I *hate* embroidered ties!"

The impassive faces of the cameramen made me think that they were not altogether "turned on" to needlework. Since they constituted my only live audience (the hollow stare of the camera was even worse!), it was not encouraging. My head bowed, I would stitch furiously away—sometimes even oblivious to the crouched figures creeping about holding large cue cards saying, "Keep it *up*." I quickly discovered this did not mean "Continue, you're doing beautifully" but "For heaven's sake, lift up your head and give us a *smile*!" I later dis-

covered that in spite of their severe demeanor (they were concentrating on *their* work, as I was on mine), the stage crew was interested and really paid attention to everything that went on, as I gathered from the questions they asked after each performance. They all, in due course, either started stitching themselves or got their wives started—except on ties, perhaps.

Actually making the shows was one thing; preparing for them was another. Peggy McCleod, who became my producer, came to New York, where we worked out each week's program. Sometimes we were inspired and got carried away completely, slaving far into the night. Along with my team of one or two "slaves" I would be stitching while poor Peggy would beg, "Rehearse, rehearse." "I must just finish this stitch. Another five minutes, please." If she had not been firm enough, the rehearsals would have been *after* the shows, not before! I'll never forget the taxi driver who returned me to my hotel in Boston at four one morning (we were planning to start the next day at seven). "Three hours' sleep is *much* better than none at all!" he said.

The first shows were fifteen minutes long. "Always leave them wanting more" seemed a good rule because "they" seemed to want more. But the second series became a half-hour long. This gave me more opportunity to show museum and antique things, which in turn led to fascinating tours of exploration around New York and Boston. Doing research for the historical part of the shows was really exciting and took us to a number of unexpected places. Cora Ginsberg was one of our first "discoveries." Her house in Tarrytown is a living museum. She collects beautiful things all over the world for museums and her own shop on Madison Avenue.

Cora Ginsberg lives among the textiles she collects for private collections as well as museums, and because of this she knows and loves every one of them. Some of the most treasured and unusual ones

8

stay in her house in Tarrytown, which gives the feeling when you walk into the front hall that you are entering the world of Mark Twain. Go up the wide staircase with its plants and white banisters to the bedroom with its crewel-covered four-poster overlooking the Hudson River (the view from the window is just like one by a painter of the Hudson River school). It was Cora who lent me the full-

length white satin Persian nobleman's coat quilted alike on both sides, which inspired me to make the evening jacket on page 40; and from trunks in her attic came the Japanese No robe on page 29, which so magnificently portrays pine trees in a snowstorm.

The Brooklyn Museum, the Harvard Library, SPNEA (affectionately known as "Spinnea" because the "Society for the Preservation of New England Antiquities" was much too long, although I did have to say that on camera), the Metropolitan Museum of Art, the Lexington Historical Society, the American Indian Arts Center, Julie: Artisans' Gallery, and Ben Mildwoff were all very helpful. Kind friends from all over contributed to the

ABOVE: Erica with Cora in her Tarrytown house.

LEFT *and* OPPOSITE: Scenes from the hall and attic.

shows: Ann Coleman, Curator of Textiles at the Brooklyn Museum, helped me so much, and Mrs. Elizabeth Howe personally brought the bed with the beautiful hangings (in her family for three generations) which are now shown at the Lexington Historical Society.

My whole house was soon filled with cardboard boxes, one for each of the thirteen shows, some pathetically empty (the ones that would be used toward the end of the series), some brimming over. For each project, ideally, there would be one finished piece, one half worked, and one just begun. Then I could pull out each one and say, "How amazing. This just grew very fast!" Some viewers said they'd never seen so many unfinished pieces! Unlike cooking, where the food *can* be raw but look cooked, there are few shortcuts in needlework— hours of work have to be put into it. One large dragon, on #14 canvas, was renamed the snail because it never seemed to get anywhere.

Things I thought would never show glared on camera. Others I took hours over never showed at all. On one of the first shows, "Kaleidoscope Bargello," my able and handsome director, Russ Fortier, angled the camera slightly from the side and fairly far away, so that when I said, "Count six threads up and one thread over," I appeared to be working on a solid piece of fabric without any visible threads at all. I told him the camera must be *much* closer on the next shows. On the following show, which dealt with quilting, he did a magnificent job of bringing the camera so close that my fingers filled the screen completely. I was painfully aware of *every* flaw in my manicure as though looking not through a magnifying glass, but through a microscope. That will teach me *not* to criticize, I thought.

The Textile Study Room at the Metropolitan Museum of Art is a veritable treasure trove. If I could only get locked in there one night by accident and just open all those drawers one by one and pore over the contents! Jean Mailey, the curator there,

With Jean Mailey in the Textile Study Room at the Metropolitan Museum of Art.

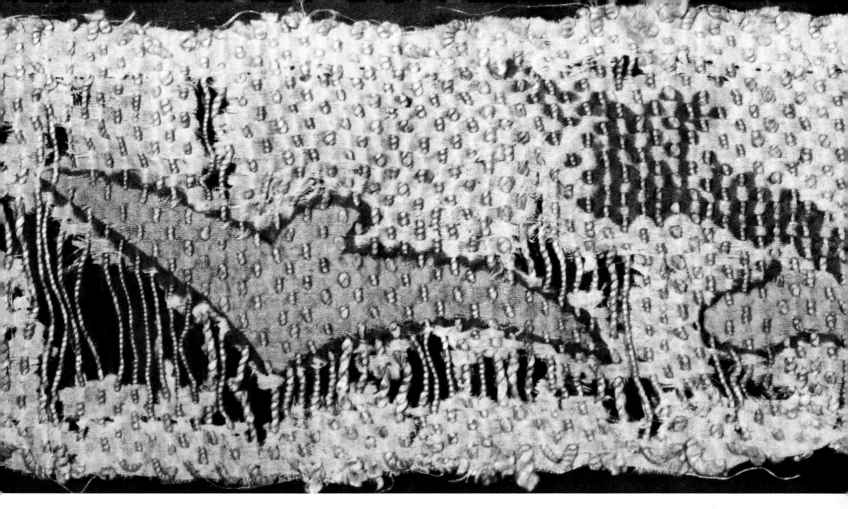

Strip with flying birds, clouds in appliqué silks, reinforced with running stitch. In shades of tan, wine, and blue on a beige-brown. Japanese, eighth century; said to be from the Horuji Period. Metropolitan Museum of Art, purchase Rogers Fund, 1944. 3¼″ x 9½″.

who presides with her enthusiastic assistant, Barbara Teague, is especially interested in Oriental fabrics and embroideries, and the collection is breathtaking. Books, samplers and American crewelwork, silk pictures—it's really like New York City itself, where I'm sure anything in the world you ask for can be produced. I was fascinated by the ancient Japanese appliqués Jean showed me (above). She explained that in China and Japan it used to be part of your religion never to throw away anything you had worn. A garment was like a part of yourself.

Therefore, everything was restored and made into something new. These very contemporary birds were torn out of old silk garments and laid down on another fabric; then the whole thing was closely stitched with running stitches for strength. Look at it closely and what do you notice? The 40 A.D. forerunner of our patchwork and quilting! (For practical warmth and necessity the early settlers in the New World also patched, pieced, and quilted their worn garments to make the lovely quilts that have become a great tradition in America today.)

Talking of quilts reminds me of my friend Ben Mildwoff, who has been collecting for years all sorts of things that at one time it was not fashionable to collect. Among these are quilts that he bought when they were relatively inexpensive and no one really noticed them. Up in the attic of his brownstone, beautifully converted into a studio, are numerous chests and boxes, each one filled with these fabric geometrics that are really works of art, and he considers them as such. One day he invited Cora Ginsberg to dinner to show her his most recent acquisition. She walked in and he unveiled it. "I won't be needing any dinner," she said. "Why not? Are you ill?" "No, it's because I just dropped dead when I saw your quilt!" she said. So from that moment, the magnificent "Garden of Eden" design, worked by Abby Bell Ross in New Jersey in 1874, has been known as the drop-dead quilt! Here it is on the opposite page, photographed with some of Ben's collection of Early American weather vanes.

Julie: Artisans' Gallery is on Madison Avenue in New York. She has a collection of clothes, sculptures, and objets d'art made by contemporary artists all over the country. An artist herself, she has a wonderful eye, and although she does not actually produce any of the things she sells, they all have a common bond because she has chosen them. Exotic feathered masks, quilted jackets, knitted and embroidered capes, soft sculpture figures, stump-work

With Ben Mildwoff, examining his quilt collection.

Opposite: "Garden of Eden" quilt with weather vanes and close-up details of the quilt.

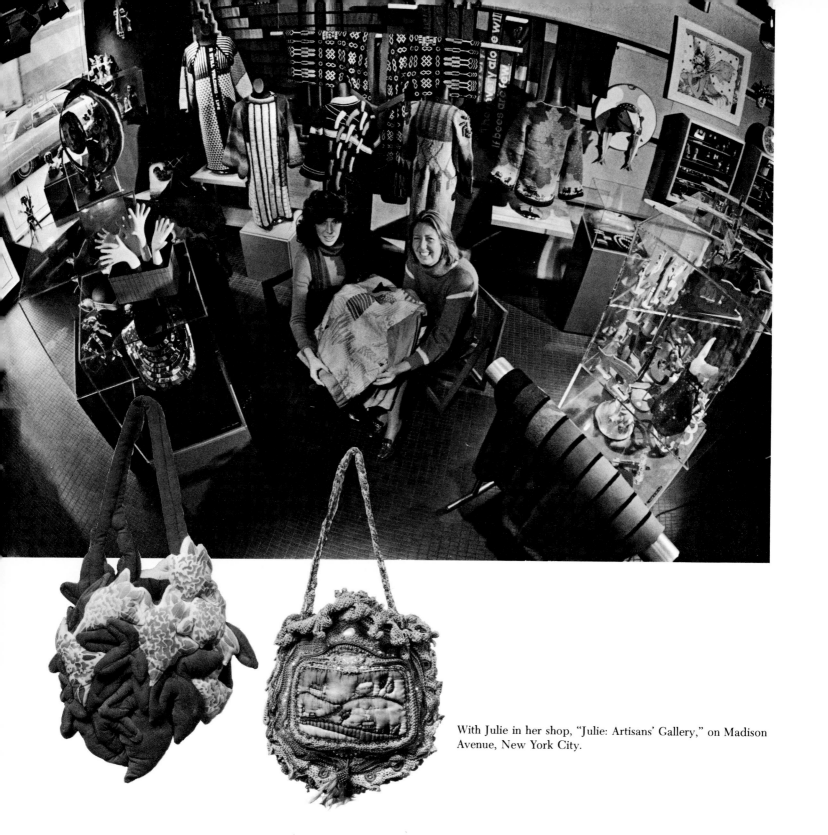

With Julie in her shop, "Julie: Artisans' Gallery," on Madison Avenue, New York City.

bags, everything is unusual, exotic, fabulous, and imaginative—and I have used some of these on my show.

I was able to produce a good deal of the needlework shown on TV by "borrowing" from my own store, too, on Madison Avenue. Not only materials, but people, too! I snatched Donna Rothchild (below) from the store to help me work on the shows; she became my right (and left!) hand and has not been allowed to return to the store since. She has taken over the running of my studio instead. On occasions, she was known to sit backstage frantically stitching a piece only a half-hour before show time. They *say* needlework makes you very calm.

Left: Donna, Erica's assistant, working on the harbor scene; and above, discussing projects in Erica's shop, just up the street from Julie's.

"Creatures Great and Small." Lion cub being stitched in the corner of the studio at 59th Street.

Once the shows were taped, recorded, and on the air, the next step was to complete all those half-finished embroideries and photograph them to make a permanent record and reference for you to follow in this book. The camera—even more than the TV camera—can make the most ordinary things look splendid and, conversely, make the most beautiful things look awful! I am therefore very critical, and may have left a trail of photographers with nervous disorders behind me—including my long-suffering husband. But if you enjoy using *More Needleplay* as much as I have enjoyed working on it, all will have been worthwhile. This is really an "ideas" book to start you thinking about some of the many exciting things you can do with needlework.

Once you begin, you will find so many other possibilities. Inspiration can come from the traditions of many countries—from Far Eastern and American Indian designs, American quilting, Scottish plaids, Russian cross stitch, French tapestry, Spanish black-and-gold embroidery, English smocking, and Japanese theater costumes. You can make such lovely things to wear and to use in your house, or create a "needle painting" as attractive as anything in oils.

Let's begin with New Points in Needlepoint—a different approach to stitching on canvas.

OPPOSITE: *"Nantucket Harbor" (instructions on page 80).*

NEW POINTS IN NEEDLEPOINT

HAVE you realized what exciting things have been happening to needle-point lately? For years we've been doing the classic continental stitch, with its beautiful, smooth tapestry shadings; but now we're taking off in all sorts of exciting new directions—crewelpoint, plaidpoint, quiltpoint. In Florida they are even doing something they call "librapoint"! All sorts of combinations of pattern, texture, and color have opened up a whole new world for us, from geometrics following the mesh of the canvas to stitches worked freely over the background without counting threads. Needlepoint artists are reconsidering their canvas and looking upon it now much as a painter looks upon *his* canvas—as a unique starting point for unlimited ideas.

On the preceding page is a harbor scene from my favorite island, Nan-tucket. I designed the scene as a collage of color, with simple graphic shapes in flat silhouette. This gives the opportunity to combine stitches and textures to help tell the story—leaf stitch creates a ready-to-burst-into-springtime tree, Gobelin stitch represents shingles and clapboard so accu-rately, and the Nantucket sea, always in motion, seems to rise right off the canvas in wave stitch.

Color page 20 (and page 21, MIDDLE RIGHT): "Lone Star" (instructions on pages 83 and 84). Color page 21: UPPER LEFT, "Log Cabin" (instructions on pages 83–85); UPPER RIGHT,

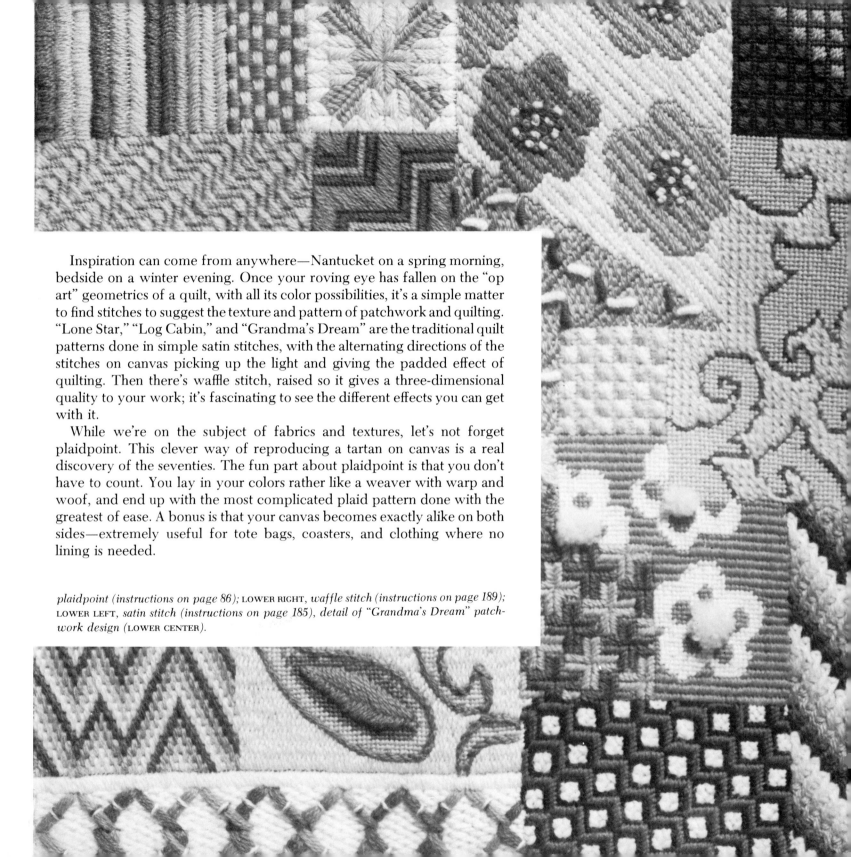

Inspiration can come from anywhere—Nantucket on a spring morning, bedside on a winter evening. Once your roving eye has fallen on the "op art" geometrics of a quilt, with all its color possibilities, it's a simple matter to find stitches to suggest the texture and pattern of patchwork and quilting. "Lone Star," "Log Cabin," and "Grandma's Dream" are the traditional quilt patterns done in simple satin stitches, with the alternating directions of the stitches on canvas picking up the light and giving the padded effect of quilting. Then there's waffle stitch, raised so it gives a three-dimensional quality to your work; it's fascinating to see the different effects you can get with it.

While we're on the subject of fabrics and textures, let's not forget plaidpoint. This clever way of reproducing a tartan on canvas is a real discovery of the seventies. The fun part about plaidpoint is that you don't have to count. You lay in your colors rather like a weaver with warp and woof, and end up with the most complicated plaid pattern done with the greatest of ease. A bonus is that your canvas becomes exactly alike on both sides—extremely useful for tote bags, coasters, and clothing where no lining is needed.

plaidpoint (instructions on page 86); LOWER RIGHT, *waffle stitch (instructions on page 189);* LOWER LEFT, *satin stitch (instructions on page 185), detail of "Grandma's Dream" patchwork design* (LOWER CENTER).

TAPESTRY

WHAT Americans call "needlepoint" the British call "tapestry." The names of this perennially popular form of stitching are constantly in dispute by purists, who say it should simply be called "needlework on canvas." They are opposed by historians, who know it all began around the sixteenth century, when the discovery of a stiffened linen mesh started a new era for needleworkers. The evenweave material, with its clearer holes and strong fine threads, made it possible to produce "paintings" on canvas with soft shadings and realistic effects, just like tapestry. Therefore, both names seem logical when you remember that "point" means stitch and so "needlepoint" means a stitched tapestry instead of a woven one.

The lovely milkmaid on this page with her benign cow is one of a pair of chair seats made in the eighteenth century. The scene was done in fine tent stitch, and because the canvas gave opportunities impossible in real tapestry, the border was worked in bold cross stitch. The contrasting textures of this sort of design are the antique counterpart to the Nantucket Harbor scene on page 17.

But supposing we look at the original inspiration once again. On the opposite page are three tapestries from Arras, the little town in France that became so famous for its weaving that in medieval times woven hangings were simply called "Arras." Instead of translating them onto canvas with tent stitches, try a new approach and lay them in long and short vertical lines to blend the contrasting colors together, in order to give the effect of a real tapestry.

On page 24 you will find my interpretation of "The Offering of the Heart," a famous medieval Arras made in the fifteenth century. When you compare my version with the real tapestries, opposite, you will see that their unique way of shading, with long strokes and strong contrasting colors, can be interpreted anew on needlepoint canvas with interesting effect. I worked with Broder Medici, that superfine wool that has been used by French weavers for centuries, but you could work in any scale, very bold or slightly finer. Because you are taking one single long stitch instead of a row of, say, six small ones, you can make a relatively large tapestry in less than a lifetime. You could use a beautiful medieval tapestry as your romantic inspiration, or design your own contemporary hanging. The whole contemporary look lies in this bold treatment, and you'll find that a change of scale and approach to stitches and color can be very exciting, using the old as a springboard to new ideas.

"Gather ye rosebuds while ye may, old time is still a-flying," my mother always used to say, quoting Robert Herrick. Instead of gathering rosebuds you can scatter them on a sofa and a rug (you'll find them on pages 25 and 90), but the time it takes won't be interminable because you can work with grospoint, using rug wool on #5 canvas. In each square of the rug you can change the four or five shades of color with each rose, yet keep the basic shape the same. In this way you can follow easily from the same graph, making each square different, and finally join them to make a large rug. Adding a square at a time makes the whole thing easy to carry about and not so enormously heavy, because you will be working on penelope canvas with half cross stitch.

Opposite: Milkmaid, eighteenth-century chair seat in needle-point, Cora Ginsberg.

Three tapestries from Arras, France: below, Vojtech Blau; at right, tapestry from the Hunt of the Unicorn series, Metropolitan Museum of Art, The Cloisters Collection, Gift of John D. Rockefeller, Jr., 1937.

Color page 24: "The Offering of the Heart" (instructions on page 89). Color page 25: Roses rug and pillows (instructions on page 90).

TREASURES
FROM THE FAR EAST

THE fabulous East has always enthralled us, ever since Marco Polo first unlocked its treasures and brought back gold and silken embroideries that Western eyes had never seen—of dragons, chrysanthemums, lotuses, and butterflies. Art in the Orient has always been part of life itself, expressing a sensuous concentration on inanimate matters together with a love of nature.

The romance of Peking, for centuries holding secrets within its moated walls, holds a special fascination for us. In the center stood the purple Forbidden City, the residence of the Emperor, removed from his people as a god would be, going back to the year 1267, when the Great Khan caused this Eden of marvelous trees, pavilions, and lakes to be formed for the "comfort and solace and delectation of his heart." The last of this long line of magic beings who lived in a dream world removed from everyday existence was the Dragon Empress Tz'u-hsi, Empress Dowager, who ruled over her celestial kingdom almost at the same time that Queen Victoria ruled over hers—for nearly fifty years.

Imagine Tz'u-hsi in the summer gardens of her palace, riding in her sedan under a huge, tasseled parasol, surrounded by her ladies and eunuchs in their scarlet, azure, and gold-emblazoned robes. Twelve court musicians were always in attendance, and whenever the Empress called for lunch, hundreds of dishes would either be cooked then and there or be brought from the palace to be set out under the trees, near which silver gray herons and azure-tiled gazebos would be mirrored in the waters of the lake. As the procession wound its way past arbors and pavilions and distant hills—which bore such names as "Pavilion of Distant Snails" and "Peak with the Wonderful Cloud Wreath"—the sound of wind bells, hung from the eaves of the temples, would be heard. Doves would have whistles tied to their tails so they sang as they passed.

Tz'u-hsi, an artist herself, had wardrobes that overflowed with hundreds of dresses, every inch worked or woven with the tiniest of almost-invisible stitches and knots. In summer the finest gauze would be embroidered with silk; in winter the robes would be lightly wadded or fur-lined.

The dragon opposite, done in gold-metal thread, is part of a royal robe. The background of silk gauze is covered completely with blue bargello brick stitches—identical on both sides.

I like to think that the green robe on page 32, which came out of Peking at the time of the rebellion in 1912—the end of Tz'u-hsi's years of splendor as well as of the old traditions of China—might have belonged to the Empress herself. It is stitched in her favorite violet silks and emblazoned with the phoenix, the female symbol of the Imperial Dragon, and with butterflies, symbols of happiness and everlasting joy.

OPPOSITE: Peking—the Summer Palace, photograph from the book *Imperial Peking* by Lin Yutang, copyright © 1961 by Elek, Ltd., reproduced by permission of Crown Publishers, New York.

To the Oriental mind repeated patterns were boring. The precise geometrics were nearly always interrupted by rhythmically flowing forms, and the effect was both harmonious and exciting. Here, the Imperial Dragon in gold thread with blue silk background on gauze. Metropolitan Museum of Art.

Color page 28: Golden needlepoint dragon encircled by clouds and waves (instructions on pages 94–99) and Chinese robe in silk and gold.

Color page 29: LEFT, *Japanese No robe;* TOP RIGHT, *gold dragon on gauze (see also below);* BOTTOM RIGHT, *Chinese robe in silk and gold. All gold thread is worked in couching stitch (see page 183).*

Details from an Oriental screen, designed by the author and worked by Mrs. John Marsh.

The "Adam" of China, P'an Ku, who was assigned to bring order into chaos, divided the universe into four sections. The tortoise, long-lived and strong-willed, controlled the north and winter. The phoenix, brilliant, full of joy and warmth of life, the south and summer. The white tiger, mature and courageous, controlled the autumn and the west; and the dragon, representing the spirit of life's renewal, and a vigilant guardian, ruled the east and spring. It is easy to see why the dragon was depicted on royal robes. Rising from the sea, with clouds above and around him, he was the intermediary—as was the Emperor—between earth and heaven. On the imperial robes nine golden dragons, each with five claws, would be embroidered on yellow silk—a color reserved for royalty.

The secrets of making both the gold and silken threads were closely guarded through the years. Silkworms, fed on mulberry leaves, would spin their cocoons. Once collected, the cocoons would be softened in water and the *continuous* filament, sometimes many miles in length, would be drawn out. The gold thread was made from real gold metal, beaten flat and stuck to thin strips of paper. This was then wrapped around a silken core, and the glowing, never-tarnishing thread was stitched on the surface of fabrics in double rows.

Besides this gold couching, the most popular Chinese stitches were silk satin stitch (often with "voided" lines or spaces between each section of stitching), long and short stitch, French knots, and the Pekinese stitch. The French knots (which should be called Chinese knots, in this case) were worked in regular rows, as many as forty to the inch. Since most Chinese embroidery was done on a frame, one hand above, one below, and the knots had to be done with *both* hands on top, they were very slow to do. A quicker method, duplicating their effect and done with an interlacing stitch, was developed in Peking's Forbidden City, which gave it its name

—Pekinese, or the "forbidden stitch." The supposition that many workers went blind doing these stitches and that therefore they were forbidden is probably incorrect. It is true that many children, starting at age eight, when their tiny, nimble fingers and good eyesight were in demand, *did* go blind at an early age. But the cruelty of this was as much a part of tradition as noblewomen's "butterfly feet" and castration to provide eunuchs—and the Chinese were probably oblivious to it. It seems logical to suppose that, just as the Royal School of Needlework in Kensington developed long and short stitch to a high degree, giving it the name "Kensington stitch," so the earlier stitch became the forbidden stitch because it emanated from Peking.

As Greece was to Rome, so China was to Japan. But although Chinese influence was strong, Japanese embroideries have their unique power and flavor. Nowhere was this embroidery developed to a greater degree of splendor than on the Nō robes, the costumes specially designed for that stately and complex Japanese theater. Walking on gleaming golden boards, the actors in their magnificent robes formed the only scenery. The pine trees in a snowstorm on page 29 show how the simple methods of couching in wool and gold thread have created a rich and dramatic effect for a Nō robe.

I used these techniques when I embroidered the panel shown at right, using as my inspiration a Japanese painting of roses dipping into a misty goldfish pool. I think that if you experiment with these techniques you will enjoy letting the elegant sophistication of Eastern tradition influence your embroidery.

Color page 32: UPPER LEFT, *silk-and-gold robe with phoenix and butterfly medallions which inspired the butterfly design for the workbox (instructions on page 93).*

Color page 33: Detail of roses from panel at right (instructions on page 100).

PATCHWORK

PATCHWORK is a way of transforming humble scraps of fabric into glorious combinations of colors. With simple geometrics you can build up sophisticated, beautiful patterns, just as our American ancestors did. They started out of necessity, because they had to re-use their worn bedspreads and clothing, and because combining patchwork with quilting made warm covers to protect them from freezing winters. But they found a miraculous transformation happened when they took the simplest geometric forms and combined them. So it's no wonder that quilts were given romantic names such as "Trip Around the World," "Sunshine and Shadow," "Grandma's Dream," or "The Rocky Road to Kansas," and became true art forms, now displayed in museums all over the world.

Try your own patchwork with simple strips of

ABOVE: Skirt in squares, vest in circles (instructions on pages 102 and 103).

Color page 36: Patchwork squares (instructions on page 102).

Color page 37: TOP LEFT *and* BOTTOM RIGHT, *yo-yos (instructions on page 103);* CENTER, *"Cathedral Windows" (instructions on page 104).*

"Cathedral Windows" (instructions on pages 104 and 105).

"yo-yos." Yo-yos are simple gathered circles which can be flattened and sewn together to make a vest or lightweight summer quilt, or strung like beads to make clowns. The ones shown opposite are my daughter Jessica's favorites. She still treasures them—they hung from her baby carriage and it seems likely that they will be passed on to the great-grandchildren!

On the next page is a tablecloth made from squares, with rows of shaded colors worked in diagonal lines. The inset shows young students beginning to quilt a patchwork quilt "top" in my garden in Nantucket. On page 37, from left to right, top to bottom, are contemporary and antique patterns —yo-yos made from batik fabrics, a Dresden plate pillow, hexagons in silks and velvets made for a quilt by my mother, an antique "sampler" quilt showing a variety of patterns, a cathedral window pattern, ribbons and velvets in a striped pattern for a pillow, an antique "pineapple pattern," "fans," and an antique silk quilt in yo-yos.

fabric—anything from borrowed (or stolen!) ties to remnants of a favorite old evening gown or to yards of bright ribbons. (See materials at right.) With a simple machine stitch, a template, and a permanent marker, you can transform your strips of fabric into an intriguing pattern in dazzling or muted colors. Quilts, pillows, evening skirts—there are endless possibilities.

After strips, there are simple squares and then more complicated circles, leading up to one of the most marvelous of all patchwork designs, called the "Cathedral Window" pattern. This is patchwork folded in such a way as to give it a three-dimensional look. The finished effect is a series of brilliantly colored stained-glass "windows" framed by the folded background material (above).

At far left, I am wearing a wraparound skirt made of squares of blue jean fabric, enriched with Guatemalan embroidery, and a vest made from

QUILTING

"How now, blown Jack! how now, quilt!" said the Prince to Falstaff in Shakespeare's *Henry IV, Part I.* In those days knights went into battle with quilted coats known as "haketons" or "jacks" under their heavy armor (could there be any connection between these and our word *jacket*?)—and more layers of quilting *over* the armor to prevent the knight from rusting in the rain or broiling in the sun. No wonder Falstaff's well-rounded form was compared to a knight already dressed for battle!

But what is quilting? It is a sandwich of two layers of fabric with padding in between. The stitching that holds all three layers together can be decorative in itself or worked in matching or contrasting color, or the quilt top can be enriched with patchwork or appliqué before the quilting is done.

As you can see from the picture on page 11, the whole thing began in the ancient Far East when old

clothing was made new by tearing the soft silk into free-form designs, laying it down onto new fabric, and reinforcing it by stitching it all over with running stitches. The Americans unwittingly followed this method centuries later when they made warm and practical bed coverings from carefully pieced old clothing. Sometimes the quilts were made from a single piece of fabric (like their English forerunners) and the quilting stitches alone formed the decoration; these were the rare and highly prized "white on white" quilts, such as the one opposite from the Smithsonian Institution. A layer of muslin was placed behind the quilt top, and the areas to be highly raised (such as the horses and carriages) were outlined and stuffed from the back. Then wadding was placed between the quilt top and a lining, and three layers were quilted together. The random stitching of the background, which contrasts the raised parts so well, is called "bunched quilting."

The first thought of the American housewife was

for a quilt that could be made quickly, so groups of ladies would gather around the quilting frame set up in the warmest part of the house and a "quilting bee" would begin. Children were paid a penny a day (worth a great deal more then than now!) to keep the needles threaded, and neighbors would often refuse to go home until a quilt was completed. Some were begun and finished in a single day with many hands at work.

As you see by the pictures here and on the following pages, quilting can take many forms. The appliqué can be outlined with parallel rows of stitching (the bird pillow in brown calicoes on white cotton). It can also be outlined with a single row of quilting to give the applied shapes a raised and padded effect (the baby quilt, pillow, and block in color on page 41). To make the stuffed quilting really raised, the shapes can be outlined with back stitch instead of running stitches (shown in the fruit basket, page 41, and known as English quilting). The shapes here were colored, using permanent felt markers, and the basket was done with parallel rows of running stitches. Thick wool was then run along these "channels" between the fabric and the muslin backing, giving an attractive corded effect. This is called Italian quilting, or "trapunto," and is the same technique as the one used for the reversible silk evening jacket on page 40. A less well-known form of quilting is "shadow quilting," shown on the tray cloth designed to match the breakfast china. The shapes are cut out in colored felt or linen or cotton fabric and sandwiched between two layers of organdy. The design is then outlined with running stitches in white cotton. Since both sides are identical, this technique is ideal for table linen or lampshades.

OPPOSITE: Quilted pillow and panel by Gladys Bolt, used by permission of Gazebo, New York.

Color page 40: Trapunto jacket (instructions on page 113).

"White on white" quilt, Smithsonian Institution.

Color page 41: Quilting techniques. UPPER LEFT, "Happy Time" crib quilt designed by Karen Jahncke; LOWER LEFT, trapunto basket; RIGHT, shadow quilting, and detail below (instructions on pages 106–17).

GAMES FOR NEEDLEPLAY

Fun and games! You'll find there are many things you can make in needlework for your favorite sport, whether it's golf, tennis, chess, backgammon, or playing cards. In fact, you may get so carried away when you start doing the needlework, you'll find it just as much fun as the game itself!

Nowadays you don't have to buy pieces of canvas and try to fit them around your golf clubs or tennis racquets—you can buy covers ready-made with a leather-backed panel of blank canvas just waiting for your artistry. The golf club covers, opposite, were done in this way with different bargello patterns on each and a large pompon in different colors for quick recognition of the club you need. You could make your tennis racquet cover in the same way, with your initials worked boldly in the center of the bargello.

The eighteenth century was one of the great ages of game playing, and some exquisite pieces of furniture were made to hold all kinds of playing boards. A friend of Martha Washington, Mercy Otis Warren, made a magnificent needlepoint card table with wild flowers around the border. I adapted her idea for the chessboard, surrounding the board with the wild flowers of the United States in crewel. You could use this border for a card table or even a mirror frame.

But talking of card tables, why not make a permanent cover for one of those folding card tables? Then you can hang the table on the wall as an attractive panel in the den and just take it down when you want to use it. So much better than trying to fit the table into a closet and having it hit you on the head when you open the door! I adapted a design from an antique set of round playing cards and worked it in bargello patterns, as you see on pages 44 and 45. You can match your colors to the room

but keep them fairly muted so that the cover is restful to play on.

Backgammon boards abound with opportunities for needleplay. A friend who is a sailor made one for his girlfriend with designs of sailboats and different-colored spinnakers in full sail for each of the points. Another friend had a husband whose favorite food was ice cream, so she worked cones in every flavor on a backgammon board for him! A very simple but colorful board can be done in bargello, as you see below, because the patterns with their V-formations fit so well into each point. And, opposite, city skyscrapers for backgammon in tones of gray and white, with a red sunset in lines of stem stitch behind, can be very effective in different stitches in needlepoint.

Why not make an Early American chessboard with free-standing needlepoint figures reenacting the War of Independence? It's a great challenge to make Martha Washington, George III, Paul Revere, Benjamin Franklin, and all the red- and blue-coated soldiers (as pawns) standing on a patchwork chessboard.

Color page 45: Card table (instructions on page 118).

Bargello backgammon board (instructions and graph on pages 120–21).

CLOCKWISE, FROM TOP LEFT: American wild flowers chessboard in crewel and patchwork; War of Independence chessboard with three-dimensional needlepoint figures (instructions on pages 124–27); sunset and skyscrapers backgammon board in needlepoint (instructions on page 120, graph on pages 122 and 123); golf club covers in bargello.

ONE-COLOR SPECTRUM

"LESS is more" has become one of the catch phrases of modern art—the idea of streamlining and stripping away anything that isn't essential and really getting down to basics. You'll find that this principle is just as true of needlework, especially where color is concerned. So take any single color—blue, brown, red, or black—and expand it into a whole spectrum of shadings with stitches.

The pillow on this page was worked in lacy delicacy on white linen, but also in shades of brown. The technique is Elizabethan black-and-gold embroidery—in this case worked in browns and beiges

Blackwork pillow (instructions on pages 128 and 130).

instead of black, but equally effective. This is one of the most intriguing forms of "one-color" embroidery, which originated in Spain before the time of Queen Elizabeth I. It's worked in a very bold and stylish manner, full of scrolly patterns reminiscent of wrought-iron work. The art was taken to England, it is said, when Catherine of Aragon married Henry VIII. To the original black, gold threads had been added, giving a richness and sparkle to the whole thing.

Blue was a favorite of Early American settlers, who made their own dyes from indigo. A whole range of different shadings could be obtained simply by leaving the fabric in the indigo pot for varying lengths of time. Limiting the design to a simple palette of blue and white can give you unlimited possibilities with texture and stitch, as you see on page 48. There, a blue bargello wing chair; a quilted appliqué bedspread in blue batik fabrics; a table mat with simple trees and a windmill in needleweaving inspired by a jacquard weave coverlet; or a wastepaper basket and hand towels for the guest bathroom, taken from the famous "Blue Onion" pattern of Meissen china . . . all are ideas to start you thinking along the lines of one color.

Other folk-art needlework has made just as lavish use of single colors, such as the Russian table linens, towels, and runners on page 49, all in cross stitch so fine and delicate it has the effect of lace appliquéd to white linen.

Brown and white is as effective a "less is more" color combination as blue and white. And you can be inspired by the simplest things—a bouquet of dried flowers, wild flowers, or even vegetables—everything from the dark brown of sorrel to the golden brown of dried artichokes and the tan of wheat stalks. I've gathered an entire palette of brown tones and combined them in a bold crewel design on oatmeal-colored fabric, then used the whole creation to cover the great wing armchair shown on page 50. The pattern of stems and leaves and birds gave me an opportunity to do all kinds of stitches—letting the strong, close herringbone of the stem be outlined with dark brown stem stitch, for example.

Whether you draw your inspiration from dried flowers, Russian aprons, blue-and-white china, or filigree Spanish blackwork, there's something about imposing limitations on your color, design, and materials that can bring out a whole group of new ideas. I know you'll discover delightful and unexpected possibilities as I did when you explore the exciting world of one color.

Color page 50: Wing chair (instructions on page 136).

Striped needlepoint pillow (instructions on page 134).

Color page 48: Batik appliqué quilt; bargello wing chair; "Summer and Winter" coverlet and "Windmill" needleweaving in white and indigo (instructions on page 132); "Blue Onion" wastebasket and hand towels (instructions on page 132).

Above: Blackwork Scherensnitte (instructions on page 128).

Below: "Windmill" needleweaving, inspired by the jacquard coverlet at above right; also see color page, opposite.

3-D COLLAGE

Let your imagination take wings, and experiment with three-dimensional embroidery. There are so many exciting ways you can raise your needlework and free it from its background: folded fabrics, stuffed and padded shapes, raised embroidery, and even sculpture in stitches. Although this may sound completely contemporary—even futuristic—it has its roots in several traditional kinds of needlework.

East Indian wedding tents have always had rosettes of folded cotton fabric in the center of the roof—a marvelous technique for petals, feathers, fish scales, or lions' manes! And in eighteenth-century England "stump work" was all the rage. This embossed embroidery in relief, which made such fascinating mirror frames or jewel boxes, can inspire us today to sew semiprecious stones, gold thread, and fine needlepoint onto our embroidery linen, or even to sculpt faces in soft muslin with features in embroidery floss and turkey work "hair."

The Victorians, always so quick to adapt old styles and techniques, had their own favorite kind of 3-D embroidery called "raised wool." It was done with wire and all sorts of wool thread. In fact, the Victorians loved this kind of work so much that they even had special sheep bred for the soft wool that was easiest to manipulate when making these raised pictures. (Unfortunately, the moths absolutely adored this wool and often penetrated the sealed shadowbox frames to take up a peaceful, undisturbed residence there!)

Using a less tasty kind of wool, but taking the rest of my inspiration from Victorian wool pictures, I made a shadowbox picture (shown at left) and put in all sorts of raised stitches. I made the petals with pipe cleaners, completely concealed beneath the woven stitch. The real fun was working with the brushed wool stitch, because it involves actually brushing the stitch with a wiry hairbrush until it becomes soft and silky and quite unlike yarn at all. The pansies on page 55 were done with this fascinating stitch.

But padding and brushing and stuffing aren't the whole 3-D story. You can work with appliqué, making a collage of needlepoint, crewel, and padded shapes, and adding crochet or even padded nylon stockings. Three-dimensional embroidery requires a sense of humor and a lot of imagination. On page 55 I am wearing a quilted dress with a belt made of clasped hands in the same material. (As I always say, it's so useful to have that second pair of hands, especially around Christmas time!) Once you start using fabrics for your raised needlework, take a tip from sculpture and try to "realize" your work all around. Cut out the shapes in muslin, pad them, and hold them together with masking tape, cutting and molding until it seems just right. Then you'll know what size your pattern has to be and just where to put in those "special effects" that give this kind of needlework its unique flavor.

Fabric-covered black-and-white tissue box with flower in East Indian folded technique.

Color page 54 (and opposite*): Floral bouquet (instructions on page 141);* top, *"Elizabethan Lady" with eighteenth-century stump-work box,* below, *that inspired it (instructions on page 138).*

Color page 55: "Hands" dress (instructions on pages 142 and 143); soft-sculpture angel faces by Elizabeth Gurrier; brushed-wool pansies (instructions on page 139).

FUN AND FASHION

DRESSING up—haven't we all loved it ever since we were children? And there's nothing more satisfactory than being complimented on what you are wearing, unless it's being able to say, "Oh, yes, it's just a little thing I whipped up myself."

Now that today's fashion and the folk wear from the traditions of every country are coming closer and closer together, we are appreciating more than ever the classic quality of handmade, hand-embroidered clothing. Vibrant colors, beautiful natural fibers and fabrics, patterns cut without a single curve to interrupt the clean lines—these can be handed down from generation to generation without ever losing their style.

The English smock I am wearing opposite is this sort of garment. Few people realize it, but the smock was once as universal in England as blue jeans are in America today. Lightweight, elastic, warm, and waterproof, it was the ideal thing for farmers working in the fields—in fact, the fabric it was made from has given us today's gabardine raincoat! Now we're smocking once again. As well as familiar children's dresses (my daughter, Vanessa, is wearing one, smocked with bullion knots, on color page 58), we're making classic English smocks, beautiful chiffon blouses, skirts, coats, jackets in lightweight fabrics.

On the subject of blue jeans, I have a favorite pair of overalls I always wear for gardening in Nantucket. And I thought the most suitable decoration for them would be—yes, you guessed it—weeds! Poison ivy is twisting up the back of one leg; dandelions, which decorate our lawn, are on my right hip; and just to give some concession to the "real" flowers, delphiniums and lupins—which grow wild behind the house—are on the front of both legs.

What did we ever do without the wraparound skirt? My natural linen one needed decorating, so I added patch pockets with a simple design in "homespun" wools—rust, teal, blue, brown, and gray-green. A coordinating shawl with the same embroidery would give me a complete costume I could wear at any time of day—and wouldn't take long to do (if only I had a few more minutes in each day!).

Another classic garment is the harpooner's shirt descended from whaling days in Nantucket. It's made of heavy homespun cotton, which is warm and interestingly textured. Imitating scrimshaw, I put a whaling scene on the back in black-and-white cotton thread. And while we're still in Nantucket, what about the shorts made by my friend Pudge Thompson for my husband, Vladimir? She appliquéd with great originality all Vladdie's favorite Nantucket "toys"—his sailboats, his Jeep, his Model T, the weeds in the garden, and even a map of the island. He adores the shorts because they are made just for him—nobody could have given him a better gift. They are shown at the top of color page 59.

Ideas in fashion would take a whole book in themselves; but just to get you started, there are several ideas on the following pages.

Color page 58 (and OPPOSITE*): Smocking (instructions on pages 144-47); poncho needleweaving,* UPPER RIGHT *and on page 73 (instructions on page 132).*

Color page 59: CENTER, *harpooner's shirt (instructions on page 151);* LEFT, *blue jeans (instructions on page 148);* LOWER RIGHT, *smocking.*

FROM THE GARDEN

Before gardens were formal and laid out with great splendor in England, vegetables used to be planted in front of the house—until one writer complained that the smell of onions was not pleasant and they should be relegated to the back. But vegetables can be beautiful. You could sketch some when you come back from the supermarket (while the ice cream melts on the kitchen table!); then you could make a recipe file in crewel stitches.

When you take your inspiration from nature, you soon learn that forms, colors, and scale all provide a bewildering variety of possibilities. So perhaps it's best to start simply, with one form repeated in mass over the entire area of your material. That's how I began the field of blossoms on page 62, working all the flowers in the same stitch—the straight stitch, which could not be simpler. I radiated the stitches into the center to get a raised, sculptured look, working with heavy threads.

From making this kind of flower embroidery to following an actual oil painting of flowers is only a short leap, because it's really just like painting with your needle. You'll soon find that you can stitch your colors right on top of one another to get the desired shading, just as though you were working with a brush, laying the colors in as you go.

You will find that flowers provide inspiration for so many forms of needlework—bold or fine crewel, needlepoint, or crewelpoint. Experiment with the ideas shown on color pages 62 and 63, using the stitches on pages 182 to 191.

So gardens and embroidery, as you see, have a long history of "togetherness," and you're really working in a long tradition when you garden with stitches. There's a bonus, too—for the flowers you make will last all year round!

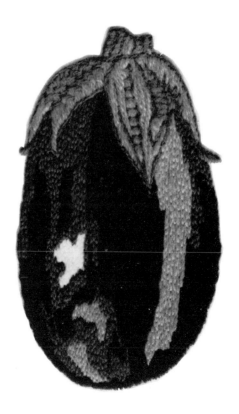

Vegetables (instructions on page 152).

Color pages 62 and 63: TOP, LEFT TO RIGHT: *"Country Life" crewel sampler; massed flowers, designed by Laura Cadwallader; "Flowers," painting by Fantin-Latour interpreted in crewel;* BOTTOM, LEFT TO RIGHT: *eighteenth-century flowers in needlepoint; three flower paintings, stitched in silk and wool.*

KALEIDOSCOPE BARGELLO

Isn't it wonderful to see the tremendous variety of beautiful patterns you can get by looking through a kaleidoscope, formed just by a few bits of broken glass and two mirrors? And when you add to that the colors and textures of bargello (that rainbow shading on canvas, called "flame stitch," shown on the next page), then you have something very exciting.

To create the kaleidoscope effect from a "straight" bargello pattern, you simply follow the technique of a real kaleidoscope and place mirrors on the design at right angles to each other. Look into the mirrors and maneuver them about until your design appears as you want it. Then you can count it off on the canvas to form an intriguing geometric pattern, repeated on four sides, like the one shown here.

Once you have the idea that you can take any design and make it into a kaleidoscope pattern, you can break away from pure geometrics and put your mirrors on abstract shapes or fruits or flowers—or anything else you fancy. I did this with oleanders on page 67, making a sophisticated pattern from a very simple motif. You can fill the silhouette shapes with different bargello stitches or work in simple satin stitch. The background of the oleander design is worked with random bargello—a free-form way of filling the background with stitches of different lengths.

The magic of a child's toy, combined with the skill of the needleworker—kaleidoscope bargello has opened up an entirely new dimension in the world of embroidery!

Color page 66 (TOP): UPPER LEFT, *"Red Geometric" (graph on page 157);* LOWER RIGHT, *"Orange Hibiscus" pillow (graph on page 159). Color page 67: "Oleanders" (instructions on page 158).*

LEFT: Erica in hand-painted suede chaps
with an Aleutian design. OPPOSITE: On the
TV set, working on jewelry,
Cheyenne chief in crewel,
and showing feathers, bead work, mocca-
sins, and a needleweaving sampler.

NATIVE AMERICAN TREASURES

THEY were the first Americans, and today their art is the first we turn to when we want to learn how simple, natural objects and colors can inspire the artist. The Indians use everything they find around them—skins, fur, feathers, grasses, stones, and sand —turning them into objects of great beauty and making their art an integral part of their life.

Instead of imitating their designs exactly, we can take a leaf out of their book and use the natural objects we have around *us* for our embroidery. Go to the craft store and buy some jute, or to the hardware store and buy some clothesline. Then look at the Indian coiled baskets (page 70) and sew down rows of jute or clothesline on canvas with a similar pattern, using wool thread. This would give you an exciting place mat or a trivet, or would be long-wearing enough for a rug or even a stair carpet!

Perhaps the most beautiful of all Indian arts is their jewelry. Worked with silver inlaid with turquoise and lapis lazuli, the designs are simple and inspirational for the embroiderer. It seems even more irresistible to translate them into stitches when you know that the names for some designs in turquoise and silver are actually "needlepoint" and "petitpoint." Using a real turquoise attached to Ultrasuede fabric in the center, with bullion knots in radiating circles around it to represent chips of turquoise, I encircled the knots with lines of real silver metal thread, with the top of the medallion made of rows of some braid couched closely together.

The pillow on page 74, upper right, was inspired by the "channel work" necklace with it. The silver channels are all inlaid with mother-of-pearl, coral, and onyx—giving an enamellike luster to the piece. A friend of mine had received the necklace as a gift; she in turn asked me to recreate it on a pillow so that she could return her friend's great favor and give her the embroidery to remind her of the necklace. I worked on velvet and changed the direction of the silken stitches on each of the petals to get the shimmering effect of mother-of-pearl. To get a crisp outline on this kind of work, it is easiest to cut out each petal in paper or thin cardboard first, then sew over the top, exactly as in the Japanese panel on page 101. Then outline with silver metal thread to get a perfect edge.

Color page 70: UPPER LEFT, *Indian-coiled plaque and baskets;* UPPER RIGHT, *couched jute, and* LOWER LEFT, *couched clothesline (instructions for both on page 164);* LOWER RIGHT, *Aleutian pillow, detail (instructions on page 160).*

Color page 71: Cheyenne chief in crewel; geometric rug (instructions on page 162).

Up in the Aleutian Islands, west of mainland Alaska, the Aleuts have a tradition of very fine basket weaving. It really looks like needlework, so the translation is very direct. Working on canvas with natural thread, you can experiment with pulled stitches—the openwork effect that comes when you draw the thread up very tightly to form needle-made lace. (See pillow above; detail on page 70, instructions on page 160.)

At left is a beautiful rug in shades of gray and natural brown. It is aptly named "Two Gray Hills," because that is the name of the Navajo reservation it comes from. Every shade and tone of the wool from which it is woven (sheep, lamb, or goat hair) is completely natural; not a single color is dyed. Up in the top right-hand corner is a long dark line going from one side right out to the edge. This is the "let-out line." The Indians believed that in every rug they wove was a spirit, and therefore it was necessary to weave a line from the center to allow it to escape.

Using the simple geometrics of the "stepped diamonds" and crosses from the Navajo Indian rug, I made the rug above in earth tones with textured stitches. Although the design is different from the one at left, the overall effect has a similar feeling and would fit into the decorative scheme of almost any room.

You can greatly enhance any boldweave material with darning or needleweaving, using the same sort of patterns the Indians developed when weaving rugs and baskets. I wove the pale cream pattern above on the shoulders of a poncho made from blue evenweave heavy cotton, while the pattern at right is darned across the back and front of the hand-woven wool poncho, worked in black, cream, and brown on the gray-brown background. Use wool that is similar in weight to your background fabric (to get a clear-cut effect I used a single strand of knitting worsted), and use a large, blunt needle to avoid splitting the threads as you darn. Weave under and over the threads row by row, so that the pattern builds up as you go along. Simple geometric patterns can be made up most easily if you use colored pencils on graph paper. The technique is the same as the darned place mat shown on page 132, except that the design here is formed by the geometric pattern. Once you get started, you'll find there are literally hundreds of ideas, and I know you're going to be as intrigued with them as I have been.

Color page 74: LOWER LEFT, *"Needlepoint" Jewelry;* UPPER RIGHT, *channel-work jewelry (instructions for both on page 166).*

Color page 74: UPPER LEFT, *part of a Zuni Indian rug, symbolizing Mother Earth;* LOWER RIGHT, *needleweaving sampler with needlepoint jewelry case in Indian motif.*

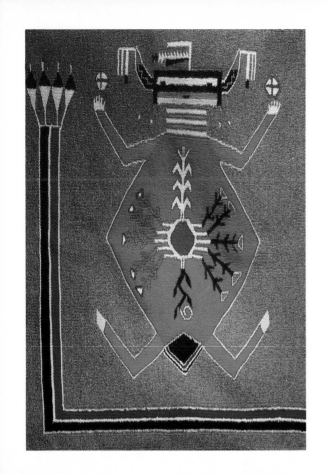

Color page 75: Centerpiece and table mat (instructions on page 168).

Color page 78: TOP, Chessie® latch hook rug, used by special permission of the Chessie System; BOTTOM, Elsa's cubs (instructions and graph on pages 174 and 175).

CREATURES GREAT AND SMALL

COME with me on a needlework safari! We'll go in search of creatures great and small and capture them all—in stitches.

Thanks to the miracles of modern technology, we don't have to wait for hours in the bush in order to sketch the animals. We have the photograph. And not only the photograph, but the photostat, so that you can transform your animals into any size or scale you want. I found a large photographic poster of Elsa's cubs and decided it would make a perfect rug, but it turned out just as beautiful when it ended up—as so many good rugs do—mounted and hanging on the wall instead of being walked on. I worked the background of jungle greens and brown shadows in long and short and random bargello on the coarse canvas. This gave a contrast of textures to the cubs themselves, whose smooth fur is simple tent stitch. When you are doing this sort of design, it's best to work on a large, square frame and from time to time to step back and see how the whole thing is growing and how it looks from a distance. Blocking in the main colors first, using permanent markers in dark, medium, and light shades of gray, is a tremendous help with the shading (pages 78 and 174).

In some ways, working in crewel, as with the raccoon on this page, is easier, because the fur can be worked just like the brush strokes of a painting. In crewel it is important to keep the flow of the stitches so that the fur looks as if it is growing smoothly, whereas in needlepoint you should simplify so that the blocks of color, and of light and shade, give you different planes. In needlepoint, your mistakes will glare at you and, unlike crewel, there is no way of covering them up. You must simply say a prayer, rip out all the stitches, and begin again!

THE TALE OF
PETER RABBIT

'Now don't get into mischief!'

'Naughty Peter went into Mr. McGregor's garden and ate lettuces, French beans, and radishes.'

He squeezed under the gate.

'Stop thief!' said Mr. McGregor. Peter hid in the watering can.

Peter was feeling sick, I'm sorry to say, so he was put to bed with camomile tea.

but Flopsy, Mopsy, and Cottentail had blackberries for supper.

The same is true of latch hooking, except that the tufts of wool can be quickly taken out and put in again. To save a great deal of time you could overlay your tracing of the photo with some semitransparent graph paper. Then the flowing lines can easily be translated into steps and blocks and the colors filled in. You will then see the exact effect of the finished needlepoint. It's much easier to erase a block of color here and there than to unpick a whole group of stitches.

In contrast to the cubs, "Chessie"® (page 78), familiar to many as the charming mascot of the Chesapeake and Ohio Railway since the 1930s, and Peter Rabbit (page 79), from Beatrix Potter's famous miniature books for children, are both "small" creatures that make interesting rugs.

Speaking of contrasts, on page 75 you have seen a whole forest full of animals, worked on organdy. I used fine cotton to stitch the winter wonderland scene in the background and then framed the piece to appear as a window. My Viennese decanter gave me the idea of working in white on white organdy to make a set of table mats and a matching centerpiece. The centerpiece is a glass cylinder that holds a floating candle. Over the cylinder an organdy sleeve is stretched, giving the subtle effect of etched glass. The whole table setting is done in shadow work, that simple but effective stitch which gives an opaque, shadowy effect on a transparent fabric.

So, wherever your safari takes you—whether to darkest Africa, the wild moonlit woods, or simply your own backyard—please don't forget to take along a needle and thread!

Color page 79: UPPER LEFT, *Peter Rabbit, latch hook rug (instructions on page 173);* UPPER RIGHT *and* BOTTOM LEFT, *Cecily Parsley and friends in crewel (instructions on page 172);* LOWER RIGHT, *"huggable" Peter in crewel (instructions on page 170). All the embroideries on color page 79 are adapted from illustrations by Beatrix Potter from the following books: rug, from* The Tale of Peter Rabbit; *two crewel embroideries, from* Cecily Parsley's Nursery Rhymes; *rabbit toy, from* The Story of a Fierce Bad Rabbit. *They are reproduced by permission of Frederick Warne and Company Limited.*

On the following pages are many of the designs shown earlier in this book. Use them by enlarging and transferring them, following the instructions on pages 176 to 180. Or simply use them for ideas, adapting the designs for your own use and experimenting with different techniques and stitches.

NEW POINTS IN NEEDLEPOINT

Nantucket Harbor Scene

THE pattern is drawn in bold outline so that you can trace it and enlarge it to any size. The original design measures 18″ x 24″ and was done with two threads of Persian wool on #14 mono canvas. You could work in any color scheme you prefer—brilliant spring colors or autumn shades, or an almost monochromatic scheme of blues, grays, and whites that would be truly Nantucket.

The idea of overlapping simple silhouettes of trees and houses could be translated to city skyscrapers or to the fields, trees, and barns of a country landscape. In this way you could interpret your own surroundings into a unique collage of color and texture.

Close-up photos on page 82 will give you ideas for combinations of stitches. Leaf stitch, of course, is the most obvious choice for a tree, but there are also fishbone, herringbone, Cretan, buttonhole, oblong cross with back stitch, and laid work, tied with cross bars. An ideal "ribbed" effect for a tree trunk is rows of stem stitch worked vertically. Stitches with the look of tiles, slate, and wood sidings are brick, Gobelin, and rows of stem stitch and buttonhole. You will find the same stitch can look entirely different if it is worked vertically or horizontally or if the scale is changed. For this reason the sky was worked in horizontal lines of split stitch, with the clouds in horizontal brick stitch, to give a smooth, calm effect in contrast to the other textures. All the stitches can be found on pages 186 to 189.

Details from Nantucket Harbor scene. For color, see page 17.

Quiltpoint—"Lone Star"

ANOTHER fascinating challenge is to capture colorful patchwork and the padded look of quilting on needlepoint canvas. On the next page you will find a diagram for the "Lone Star," a quilt design that has been handed down from generation to generation of Americans and is perhaps one of the most striking of all the traditional patterns. The star is shown in color on page 20, worked in large scale with rug wool on #7 canvas. This works out to fit into a square 30″ x 30″ and would make a magnificent rug with several squares joined together. You can see how the same star can be completely different worked in small scale and with different colors by comparing it with the one on page 21. The star was worked on #14 canvas with three strands of Persian wool, and measures 18″ x 18″.

To work a star of any size, follow the graph on page 84. Begin in the center of the design (at arrow 1) and in the center of your canvas, making a block of four vertical stitches over five threads of the mesh. (These stitches are shown by the bold, straight lines in the diagram.) Change to a new shade and work two more blocks of color immediately above the first one (shown by thin, wavy lines in the diagram). Continue, following the diagram, increasing by one block of stitches with each new row, ultimately decreasing to form the points. Then make a second diamond shape exactly like the first, but to the left of it, as shown in the diagram, working horizontally instead of vertically. Once you have worked these two points you will have formed one quarter of the star shown in the photo, and can repeat this on the other three sides. (Note: The star can be any size, depending on how many rows of color you work before decreasing to form the points.)

The diamond-pattern background is worked vertically over the entire design. Begin each diamond over two threads, increasing to ten in the center, as shown in the diagram (center right, page 84). To establish the position for the first diamond, however, it is easiest to start by fitting it exactly into the angle between the points (at arrow 2).

It is important to remember that the smallest stitch of each diamond is over two threads—not one—and that there is a space of two threads (or one hole) between diamonds. This allows the long center stitch of each one to fit up between the points, forming the diagonal crisscross effect resembling quilting, which you see in the photo.

Quiltpoint—"Log Cabin"

THIS design relies for its effect on an interesting juxtaposition of colors. The simple bands of slanting stitches resemble the log cabin patchwork, composed of joined ribbons or strips of fabric.

The design can be worked on any scale, but the one shown in color on page 21 and in the graph on page 85 was done on #12 canvas, with three threads of Persian yarn, finished size 17″ x 17″. Begin working in the center of the design (marked with an arrow on the diagram) in the center of your canvas. Start with a slanting stitch over one thread, then over two, increasing up to nine threads, and then working the band of this width all the way down (89 stitches). Complete the triangle by working ten bands of color, as in the diagram; then turn the canvas and repeat exactly from the center again. Once the four inner triangles are worked, you can work the four outer ones to get the effect of a diamond superimposed on a square, as shown in the photo.

84

RIGHT: "Lone Star," showing section enlarged in graph, BELOW. Use the symbols for placement of colors, working with your own shades; or follow color page 20. Note the arrows for the angle of background stitch.

LOWER RIGHT: "Log Cabin," showing section enlarged in graph, OPPOSITE.

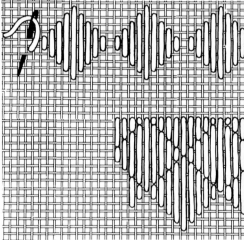

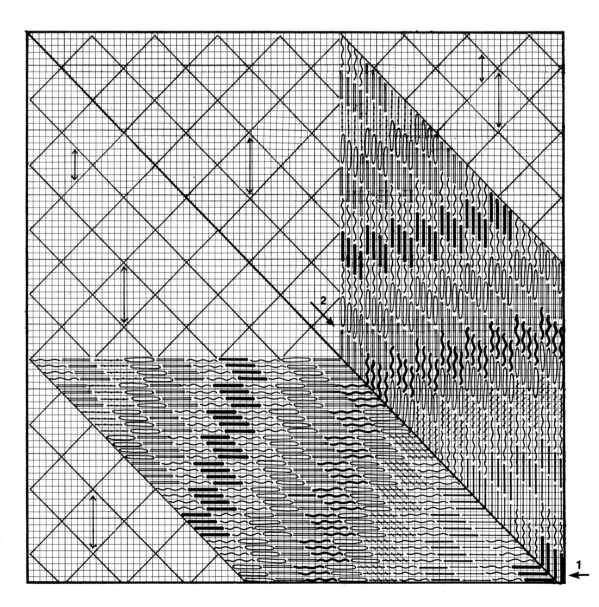

Plaidpoint

SINCE needlepoint was originally inspired by woven tapestry, it's surprising that it has taken us so long to discover other stitches on canvas that give the effect of weaving. Imitating bold, nubby, and tufted textures with "mock weaving" stitches can add new dimensions to needlepoint (see opposite). "Pulled work" is another departure, which gives an open, lacy effect (pages 160 and 161), while weaving a plaid on needlepoint canvas is definitely a "new point" of the twentieth century. At first glance you might ask how plaidpoint differs from regular needlepoint. The secret is in the method of working, which allows you to work the most complicated tartan with a minimum of counting—you count only the rows of color, not the individual stitches. It's also identical on both sides, so it's ideal for vests, handbags, and rugs.

Practice it first with only two colors so that you will quickly understand the simple principle.

PLAIDPOINT

Using a long enough thread to complete the row, come up at the top left corner of the design. Following the diagram, come up, count one thread down and one thread over to the left, and go down. Come up, level with the first stitch, leaving one thread open between.

Repeat all the way across, skipping every other stitch. Check the reverse side, and if you have worked correctly you will have the same thing on the other side (the stitches simply slant in the opposite direction).

Now work another row next to the first, placing the stitches under the spaces of the first row. Because all the stitches slant in the same direction, several rows together will form the effect of diagonal lines, as in the diagram below.

Work three rows of the first color, four rows of the second, then three rows of the first again.

Vladimir Kagan, the author's husband, in plaid vest; and BELOW, plaid rug being started on #5 canvas with rug wool.

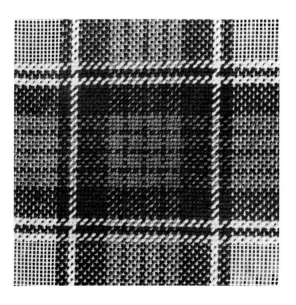

PLAIDPOINT

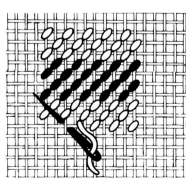
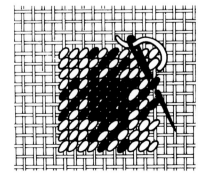

Now work all the vertical rows, repeating the horizontal rows exactly as in the diagram, using the colors in the same order. You will find that the verticals automatically fill in the spaces left by the "skipped" stitches on the horizontal rows, and when you have completed the three rows of the first color, four rows of the second, and three rows of the first again, you will have the effect of a real plaid—alike on both sides.

End off by weaving the threads invisibly back into the stitches at the end of each row.

The plaid is often enhanced by a fringe, simply leaving long threads hanging at one end of the row, trimming them evenly afterward. In working your real plaid (as opposed to your practice one), "set" the colors by working all the horizontal rows first, then repeat them exactly in the same order on the vertical rows. If you are designing your own plaid, instead of following an existing one, work the pattern out with colored pencils on graph paper first, so that you can see the finished effect before you begin.

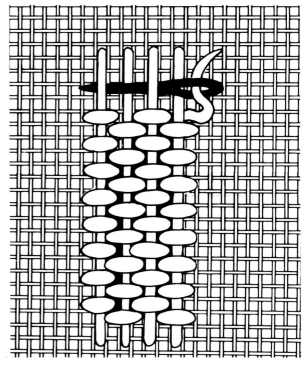

MOCK WEAVING

Pillow worked in three simple stitches—mock weaving, couching, and uncut turkey work.

Mock Weaving

WOVEN pillows in blond, ivory, cream, and silver-gray with nubby, tufted, and tweedy textures are most effective, and it's satisfactory to interpret them with simple stitches on canvas. Just like a weaver, you can let yourself go choosing wools, silks, and cottons—candy to the designing eye! Bold roving and rug wools, tweedy knitting wools with heather mixture, and shiny silks combine beautifully with stitches such as cut or uncut turkey work, fishbone, herringbone, couching, back stitch, stem stitch, and of course mock weaving itself, shown here. Work in stripes and bands of varying widths to make a pillow like the one shown at right. Once you begin, you will find the ideas coming to you as you go along. The base threads go through the canvas only on either end and the weaving threads go through only at either side—so the result is a band of real weaving on the surface of the canvas.

TAPESTRY

"The Offering of the Heart"

THE design shown opposite and in color on page 24 may be worked in any scale, using several threads of wool for a bold effect or fine canvas with cotton floss for a miniature panel. My original was done on #12 canvas, using six to eight threads of Broder Medici (fine French tapestry wool), and the finished panel measures 29″ x 38″.

The whole design is worked vertically with long and short stitches to blend the colors together and give the effect of a tapestry. Small, narrow areas are worked in satin stitch, coming up on one side, going down on the other. It is important not to change the angle of the stitches, keeping them upright, side by side, even where the design suggests a diagonal angle, such as the man's leg.

Cover the canvas completely with stitches. For instance, leave no space where the man's leg joins the background; allow the stitches to share the same holes. Then outline on top with stem stitch in a contrasting color to make a clear, crisp edge. In the same way, the grasses on the forest floor and facial features are best worked right on top of the stitching to make clear, smooth-flowing lines. The long and short tapestry stitch (or random bargello) is shown here and is used for all the main areas of the design. Instead of using this stitch for the leaves and ground, you can work as shown in the second diagram at right. Here the short stitch fits the shape and the long stitch extends on either side, as shown. This makes even the most strongly contrasted colors blend softly together.

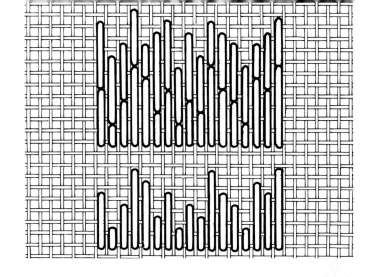

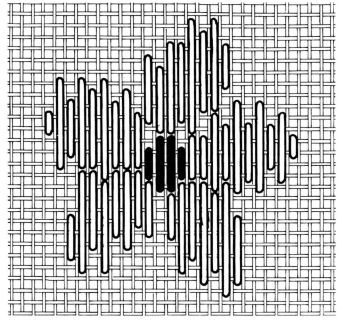

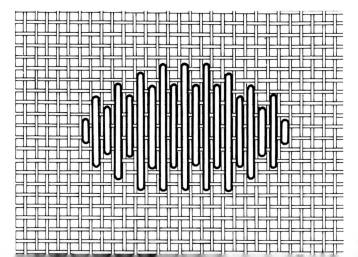

TOP: Long and short stitches for tapestry effect on canvas; BELOW, two diagrams showing flowers and ground in tapestry stitch for the "Offering of the Heart" panel.

squares together on the sewing machine to make strips, and then join the strips to form the rug. Open the seams and press flat; line the rug with coarse linen or rug backing. Close-textured backing is not recommended, since the dirt will be trapped inside the rug and cut the stitches.

Victorian Roses

THE Victorian roses shown here as a sofa, as pillows, and as a rug have a contemporary look because of their bold scale. They were worked in rug wool on #5 canvas. As you see in the color picture on page 25, each square is surrounded by a geometric border, so that when the squares are joined into a rug, an interlocking design is formed, linking the sprays of roses together.

Because each of the four roses is worked in four or five shades of one color, you can rotate the colors, making the deep red rose of one design pale pink in the next, and so on—giving each square of the rug a completely different look, yet keeping an overall balance. Work the design in half cross stitch (page 186), because it will be lighter and quicker to work on the large-scale rug canvas. You can count the design out, working in horizontal rows across the design—or you can pick out the main elements, counting it out rose by rose, working the leaves last. Before joining the squares for the rug, block each one carefully (page 181), since it is essential that they should be square to make neat joins. Seam the

COLOR KEYS

1. *Pink rose*

- ⊡ Pale pink
- ◩ Bright pink
- ⊠ Deep pink
- ▶ Magenta
- ⊙ Rust

2. *Yellow rose*

- ⊡ Pale yellow
- ◩ Bright yellow
- ⊠ Gold
- ◼ Dark gold (rust)

3. *Red rose*

- ◩ Medium peach
- ⊠ Bright red
- ▶ Red-purple (aubergine)
- ⊙ Black

4. *White rose*

- ⊡ White
- ◩ Cream
- ⊠ Light beige
- ▶ Warm beige
- ⊙ Brown
- ◼ Rust
- ◿ Yellow
- ◺ Avocado

Leaves

- ⊡ Cream
- ↗ Light brown
- ⊞ Light green
- ⊞ Dark green
- ◺ Light olive
- § Olive
- ◩ Dark olive

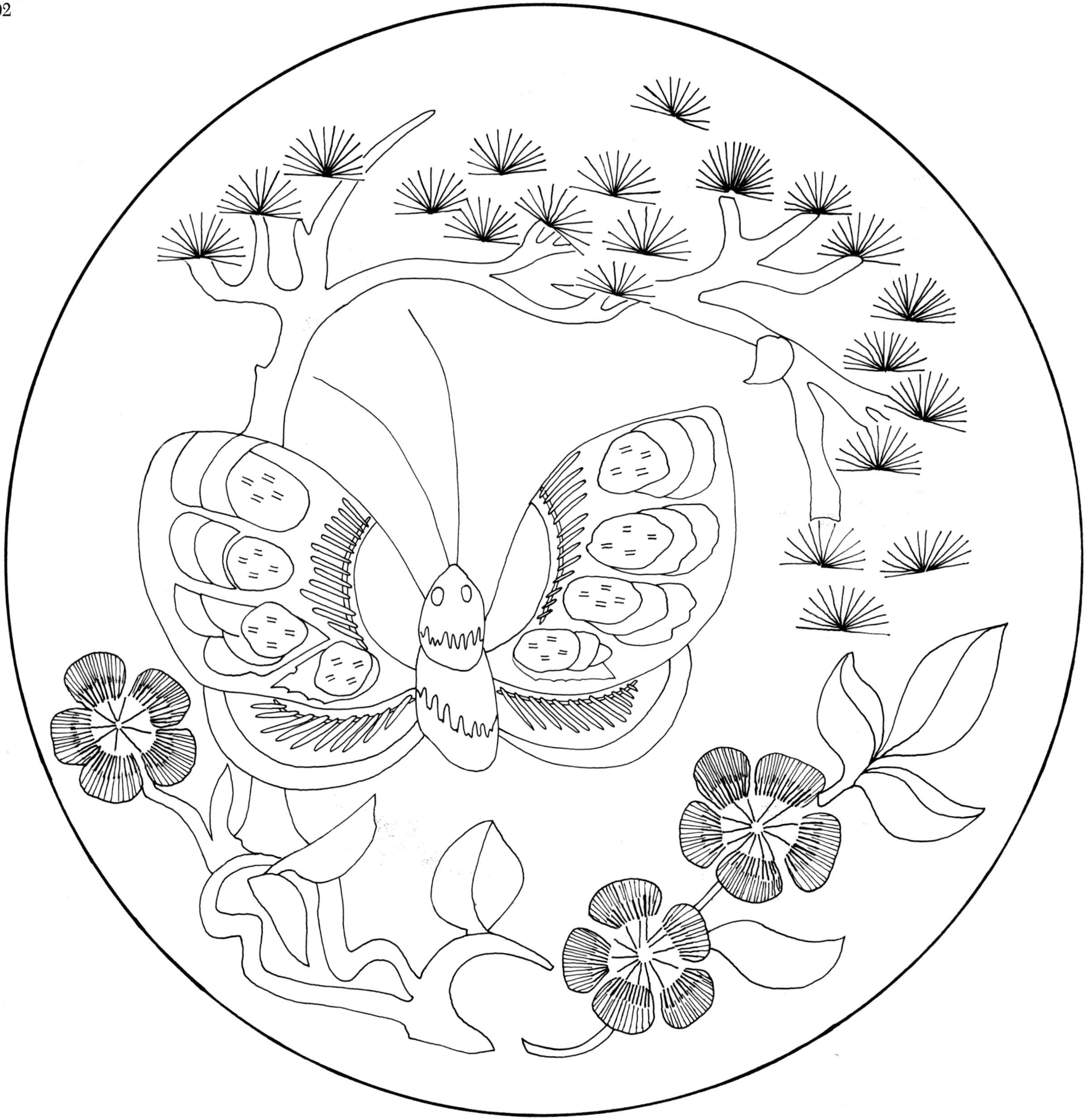

TREASURES FROM THE FAR EAST

Butterfly

THE green robe from the Imperial Court of Peking (shown on page 32) is exquisitely worked with medallions of fine silk embroidery, each one enclosing a phoenix, a bird of paradise, or a butterfly. I used the butterfly design as a centerpiece for my mother's workbox (shown in color on the same page), and in working it on brocade I learned quite a few Oriental secrets—ways of making simple stitches most effective. They are shown here. You can trace the butterfly and pine tree from the life-size outline on the opposite page and transfer it in any size to any material you prefer (see pages 176 and 177). My original was done in real silk floss with gold metal threads on damask, and measures 8″ in diameter. The circle enclosing the whole design is done in Pekinese stitch.

The pine needles are straight stitches radiating into one central hole. The blossoms are long and short with straight stitches worked over the top afterward, again into one hole in the center. The butterflies' wings are straight stitches with another thread woven underneath afterward to raise them. The butterflies' antennae are whipped chain. With silk thread, work a line of chain stitch, keeping the stitches small. Using a blunt needle, slide under each chain stitch, using metal thread. Do not pass through the fabric except at either end of the line.

PEKINESE STITCH

First work a line of back stitch in silk thread. Then, using a blunt needle and a short length of gold metal thread, interweave the back stitch as shown. The final effect looks like a gold braid laid down on the fabric.

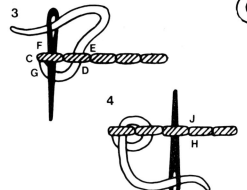

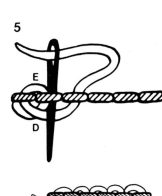

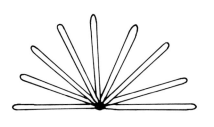

Pine needles

Blossoms

Butterfly wings

Butterfly antennae

Dragon

In the photos above I am working the butterfly design and wearing the robe from which it was taken. In contrast is the dragon, shown on the opposite page, and in color on page 28. The complete dragon panel measures 36″ x 36″ and was done on #14 canvas in wool with silk and metal threads. If this sounds like an ambitious project, you may feel better when you know that the central circle measures only 24″ x 24″, and that the panel was designed to be a worked circle on a square of *painted* canvas. This is an interesting way of framing a picture, with the mat, or surrounding part, of the same material as the picture itself. If you prefer, instead of painting the surrounding canvas you could work it in a contrasting color using the same stitch you used in the design, or in a bolder one to provide texture. The whole design was worked in tent stitch (the basic needlepoint stitch shown on page 186) and may be counted out from the graphs on the following pages. Instead of the vivid Oriental shades shown on page 28, you could use a palette of brown, oatmeal, camel, cream, and white, which would be a foil for the sparkling gold thread of the dragon.

Burden stitch (left) is an effective way of making the dragon scales, using cotton floss underneath and aluminum-based gold Lurex on top—as you see in the photograph opposite. Start by outlining the dragon with tent stitch in dark gold. Then work the burden stitch within the area, working the basic horizontal bars in floss, two threads apart. The metal thread, fitting over them, will then be in vertical stitches of four threads deep. A more subtle effect, showing less gold thread, if desired, is to work the horizontal bars of gold thread first, overlaying them with vertical stitches in cotton floss or silk.

Graphs for working the dragon are on pages 96–99.

BURDEN STITCH

"Roses Dipping into a Misty Pool"

You can heighten the romance of an eighteenth-century Japanese painting on silk by translating it into stitches on beige velvet, using white wool, green silks, and gold metal threads. Anyone who has attempted to work on velvet knows that it is extremely hard to keep the edges of shapes crisp and clear, because the texture of the velvet defies evenness—it's almost like working on fur. To make life easier, first stretch the velvet in a square frame, then cut out each leaf shape in thin cardboard (postcard weight) and stitch it down all around, as in the diagram opposite. You can then work silken satin stitches over this base with the utmost smoothness. Work in the Oriental manner with a "voided" line to show the vein—in other words, a separation between the two sections of leaf where the background fabric is allowed to show through. The design is shown in color on page 33. It may be enlarged and transferred following the instructions on page 176.

ORIENTAL SATIN STITCH

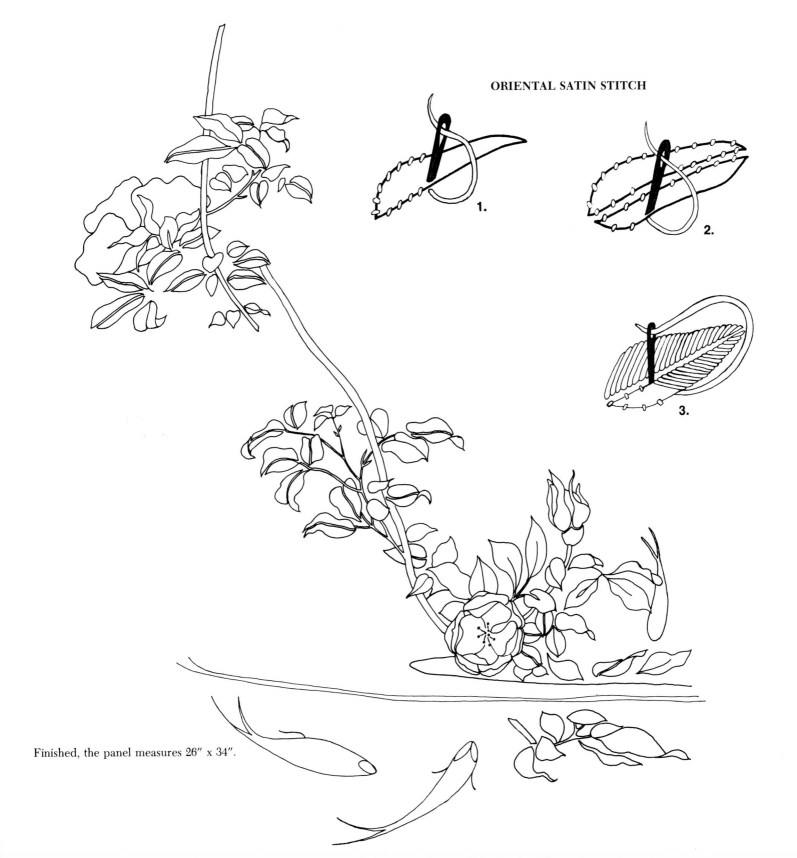

1.

2.

3.

Finished, the panel measures 26″ x 34″.

PATCHWORK

Squares

THE simplest shape to make in patchwork is a square. When I prepared my television shows, I thought naively that the simplest pattern to make would be diagonal bands formed from rainbows of different-colored squares, as illustrated in color on page 36. This is in fact quite difficult, unless you are *very* careful and *very* accurate. If your squares are of slightly different sizes, then your diagonals suddenly turn into checkerboards!

So, to keep each square identical in size, start by making a template, or pattern. Cut out a square in graph paper 2″ x 2″ and glue this to a square of cardboard cut from a tissue box or postcard, or something of similar weight. (You can also buy metal templates from needlework stores, which will outlast the cardboard ones.) Draw around this shape in brown paper and cut several out, being careful to keep them all precisely the same. These brown paper squares are your working patterns. Lay them on the straight of the fabric, spacing them apart to allow for turnbacks on the fabric, and baste each one in position with a single stitch to catch it in the center. Now cut out the fabric with ⅜″ turnbacks all around, and go to the ironing board. There you can carefully press the turnbacks accurately over the brown paper, stacking up the squares as you go to make sure they are the same size. If your pressing was accurate, you may leave out the basting step shown here, and simply oversew the pieces together. Oversew these, right sides facing, as in the diagram here, sewing them together in strips in the color sequence you have chosen, in the length you require. The next strip should be in the same sequence except that the first color square is now moved to the last position in the row. Step down the colors row by row in this fashion, until you have completed enough strips for the width of your piece. (Keep checking for accuracy in size and placement of colors as you go.) Pull out the brown papers and basting stitches as each row is finished. For strength and evenness, press the

1.   **2.**

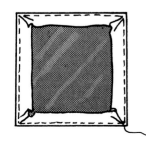

3.

Squares: (1) template laid on fabric; (2) fabric basted to brown paper pattern; (3) squares being joined by over-sewing.

turnbacks of each square alternately to left and right instead of all to one side. You can quilt this design as on page 106 or leave it unquilted to use as a tablecloth, backing or lining it with a contrasting fabric.

Circles (Yo-Yos)

Like the squares, circles call for extreme accuracy. If each one is not exactly the same size, joining them will be next to impossible. An excellent way of using up your inaccurate circles is threading them on strings like giant beads to make a clown, as shown below!

The procedure is exactly the same for circles as for squares, except that your finished circle will be half the size of your template, so you must allow for that. To keep perfect curves, cut out fabric and brown-paper patterns with curved scissors. Follow the diagram below, turning the fabric over the brown-paper pattern and running a row of tiny stitches round close to the edge. Pull out the brown-paper pattern and draw the running stitches up tightly. Secure the thread firmly and press the gathered circle of fabric flat. Now, just as you did the squares, join the circles together in strips, in the color sequence you prefer. Join them by holding the circles together, right sides facing, taking several oversewing stitches close together to hold them firmly. To make a vest, pin strips of the correct length face downward on top of a paper pattern and oversew the strips together while they are still pinned down. This will ensure a good fit.

Yo-yos: (1) running stitches around edge; (2) pattern removed, shape being drawn up; (3) completed yo-yo; (4) yo-yos being threaded to make clowns, as shown at RIGHT.

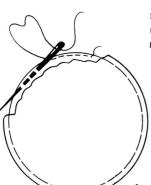

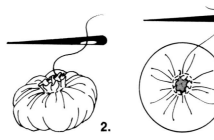

1.　　**2.**　　**3.**　　**4.**

"Cathedral Window"

THIS intriguing quilting pattern has a three-dimensional effect made by folding the fabric. The pattern is based on squares, and as the final square ends up being one-quarter of the size it started out, you must allow for this when cutting your pattern. Each finished square of the pillow shown here measures 3″ x 3″; therefore, the pattern cut in graph paper measures 6″ x 6″.

"Cathedral Window" pillows. The completed pillow AT LEFT is decorated with "biscuit puffs"—little circles of gathered, padded fabric sewn down at each intersection.

Start by gluing graph paper to cardboard, to cut a perfect square. Place this pattern (template) on the fabric and trace around it exactly with a pencil. Cut out the shape, leaving ½″ extra on all sides. (You must cut nine of these squares to make the pillow shown here.)

1. Now, placing the template on top of your cut-out square (penciled lines facing you), run a steam iron over the straight edges of the template with the

extra half-inch of fabric folded on top of it. When you lift out the cardboard, you will have a perfect square of fabric with turnbacks creased, as shown in the diagram opposite.

2. Fold it in half (with turnbacks facing) and stitch each side together between the arrows, as in the diagram. When it is stitched, pull it open at the crosses and flatten it out to a diamond shape.

3. Now sew together with an overcast stitch between the arrows (don't catch these stitches to the back of the fabric).

4. Fold each of the four points to the reverse side; the dotted lines in the diagram show where to fold.

5. This diagram shows the folding in progress. Catch all four flaps firmly together in the center (again, don't stitch the back of the fabric).

6. Now start joining squares with the blind stitch. You must join at least four before you can form your first "window."

7. Finally, take a small square of printed fabric and place it on the folded fabric, as shown by the shaded area in the diagram. Catch it in place, then fold back the four bordering edges of the original fabric to form a rolled frame overlapping the contrasting diamond all around. Hold the rolled edges in place by catching them together at the four corners. This gives the lovely three-dimensional effect. Repeat with different fabric on each of the other diamonds.

BLIND STITCH

1. Working on the right side, slide the needle into the fold first above and then below the seam.
2. Pull firmly, and the small stitches will become invisible.

BLIND STITCH

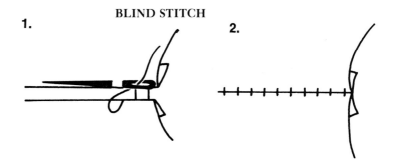

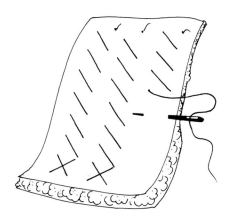

BASTING STITCH

Basting quilt top, batting, and lining together to form a "sandwich." Note wide basting stitch, excellent for holding fabrics firm.

Quilting on a round frame. The fabric is loose, so four to five stitches can be taken at one time on the needle. Note position of forefinger of left hand.

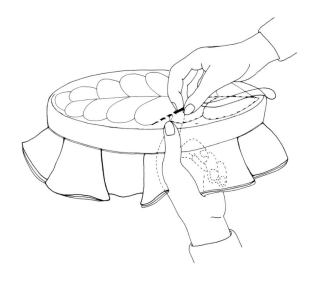

QUILTER'S KNOT

1. Take a tiny stitch, leaving a tag hanging out of the fabric.
2. Take another tiny stitch in the opposite direction from the first; twist the thread to form a loop and slip it over the needle, as shown in the diagram.
3. Pull through to form a tight knot.

QUILTING

Basic Steps

QUILTING—a way of sandwiching three pieces of fabric together—can be done in several ways. The most basic quilting is done with running stitches in simple geometric patterns on a plain fabric, or following the design of an appliqué or patchwork quilt. Close, random all-over stitching is sometimes an effective contrast. Called bunched quilting, it is shown on the quilt opposite.

Soft fabrics are best for quilting, so that the finished quilt will be light and airy; among the best are cotton, Dacron, crepe de chine, fine muslins, or batiste. (Heavy fabrics flatten the batting or filling and reduce the warmth.) Use waxed quilting thread for strength and quilting needles that are short and strong, making even stitching possible.

Begin by basting the quilt top, batting, and base fabric together so that they can be worked as one. Lightly stretch the lining face downward, into a square frame. Lay the batting on top and then the quilt top, and baste the three layers together as shown. Cut out simple shapes (some basic ones are shown on pages 108–9) as quilting templates in nonslip sandpaper, and outline them with tailor's chalk on the quilt top. (Tailor's chalk pencils are available in several colors for light or dark fabrics.) Hard (H) pencils make accurate markings, but are often difficult to eradicate when the quilting is done. Experienced quilters stretch the fabric tightly in the frame, lay the template down in the correct posi-

1.   **2.**      **3.**

tion, and scratch the fabric with a needle, marking the design in this way a little at a time as they sew.

You can begin with a knot, pulling the thread sharply so the knot disappears between the layers of fabric and stays buried in the wadding, or you can use the quilter's knot shown at left, which starts your thread firmly and invisibly with the first stitch. End off by running back into the wadding between the layers, again burying the thread invisibly. The stitching itself is very simple—a running stitch with the spaces between the stitches equal to the stitches themselves. With the fabric stretched loosely in the frame, you can take four or five stitches at a time with the short, strong quilting needle. You must hold one hand always under the frame to guide the needle and help push it upward, while the other hand on top does the stitching. Some quilters wear a leather finger guard, half-thimble, or rubber thimble on the hand under the frame; others prefer to feel the needle and work without protection. Making the stitch as clear on the underside as it is on top takes practice, but starting with thin wadding, such as a thin blanket, makes it easier to develop speed, rhythm, and evenness.

Eighteenth-century "white on white" quilt with "bunched" background stitching to accentuate the padded figures. Smithsonian Institution.

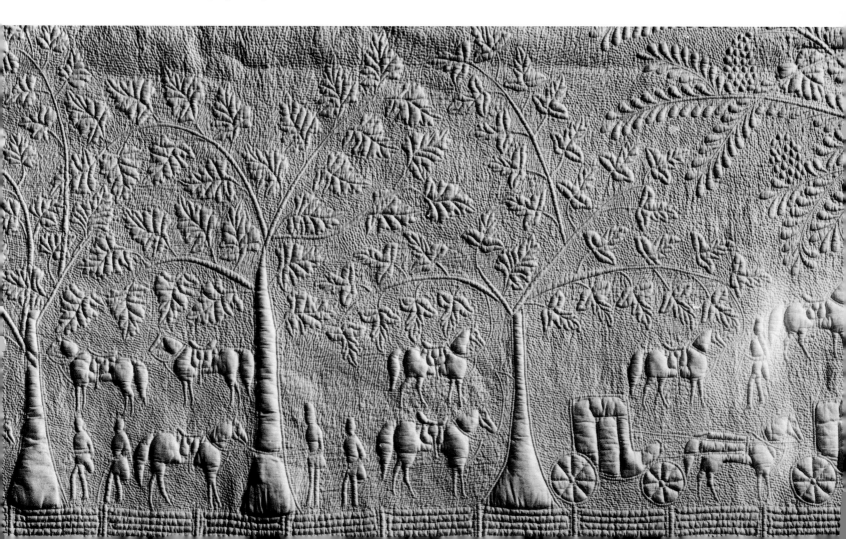

Some English quilting templates. See previous page.

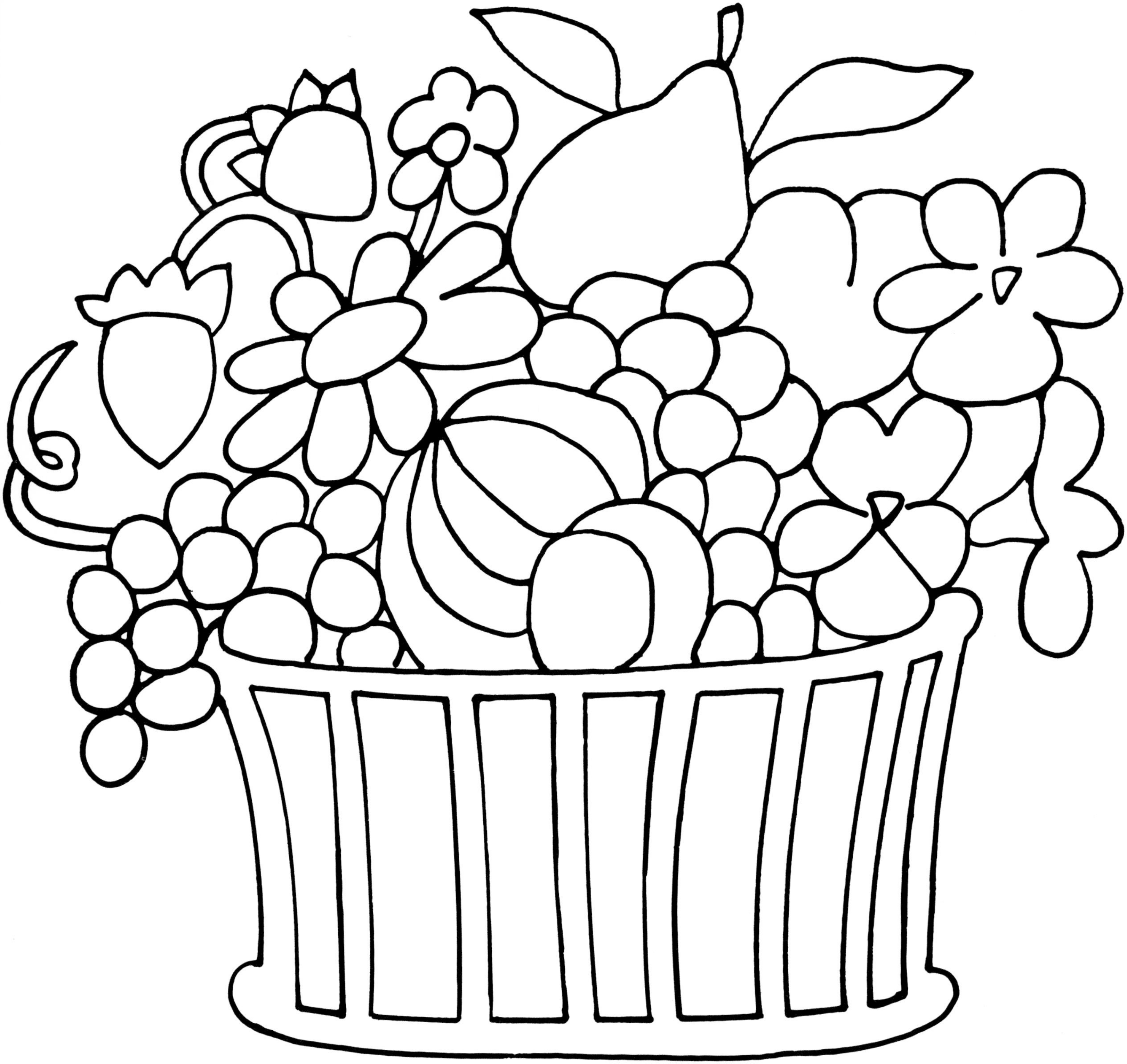

Stuffed, or Padded, Quilting

QUILTING can also be padded by stuffing from the back. In the bedspread from the Smithsonian on page 107 this kind of padding was combined with ordinary quilting to raise and accentuate parts of the design. To make the basket of fruit, shown opposite and in color on page 41, first trace the pattern on muslin or soft, sheer fabric to serve as a backing. Then select any material suitable for quilting, such as soft cotton, silk, or satin (the original basket was done on natural polished cotton). Next, baste the two fabrics together, as shown in the diagram on page 106, covering the whole area with stitches, working across the design as though it were not there. This will hold the two fabrics together as though they were one.

Now, working on the reverse side, outline the whole design with running or back stitch. Because you are working on the reverse, if you decide to use back stitch you must actually use stem stitch—which results in a back stitch on the front.

When the stitching is complete, remove the basting stitches and carefully cut a small slit in the backing of each section on the reverse side, as shown below. (It is helpful first to separate the two fabrics with two crossed pins, to avoid accidentally snipping the fabric on the right side.) Then stuff the shape with Dacron batting or resilient lamb's wool, pushing the pieces well up into the corners. The stuffing should always be light, not pushed in so tightly that the padding becomes heavy and hard. Lightly catch the slits together at the back, and finish with a lining.

In the basket opposite, the design, measuring 16″ x 20″, was done with back stitch on polished cotton, and the shapes were colored with felt fabric markers. Permanent markers available for fabric allow you to add color to a design very simply but the design is equally effective uncolored. The basket banding was too narrow to pad like the rest of the design, so four strands of bulky Nantuk (a thick, lightweight Orlon fiber) were threaded between the lines of stitching. Called trapunto, or Italian quilting, it is described on the next pages.

  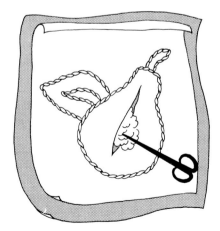

(1) Reverse side, showing stem stitch outline (back stitch on the front); (2) reverse side, showing slit being made in muslin (pins prevent accidental cutting of front fabric); (3) reverse side, showing stuffing.

Italian Quilting, or Trapunto

THE jacket shown in color on page 40 is an example of Italian quilting, or trapunto. In this type of quilting, thick wool threads form the padding, which is run between the two fabrics *after* they have been stitched together in a channel design. Trapunto is usually done on a soft, silky material with a muslin backing that is lined afterward, but it may also be done with "good" fabric on both sides so that it is reversible. This is the way my evening jacket was made, inspired by a full-length satin Persian nobleman's coat made in the eighteenth century. I chose real silk fabric in rose on one side and beige on the other, and stitched in matching rose thread (three threads DMC cotton) so the pattern was clearly delineated on the beige side.

In choosing a fabric, the essential thing to look for is a soft, pliable material, so that the holes made by the large needle for stuffing will readily close up again, making the method of padding invisible. Satin, silk, polished cotton, and fine linen are all suitable materials. Once you have the fabric, find a pattern and cut the whole jacket out in muslin. Baste it together and fit it, stitching up the darts. Once the pattern fits, take it apart, cut it out in fabric, make it up, line it, and trace the design with dressmaker's carbon (see page 178) all over one side. Start in the center back, making sure both sides of the pattern are balanced, continuing the pattern right across the seams. The border shown here (page 112, right) can be traced all around the back and up the front. Using even stitches, run along all the outlines of the design using quilting thread or DMC cotton. Work an average of seven stitches to the inch. Then, using a blunt tapestry needle, thread through the channels with three or four strands of soft Dacron, cotton, or wool yarn. Pierce only the top layer of fabric, drawing the thread lightly between the stitched lines and taking as long a stitch as is comfortable. Pull through, return to the same hole, and pull through again. As you go, stretch the fabric firmly in different directions to take up as much thread as possible in the channel. Stroke the hole together so that there is no trace of where the needle returned each time.

OPPOSITE: Repeat overall pattern for trapunto jacket. Border for collar, cuffs, and around jacket should be enlarged to a 4-inch width with straight border lines on either side, as in the photo.

Appliqué and Quilting

THE "Happy Time" child's quilt shown on page 41 is done with applied fabrics such as calico and gingham and lightweight plain cotton. The quilting surrounds each motif with small running stitches, making the patterns stand out clearly with a padded effect.

Enlarge and cut out the paper patterns of each of the shapes and motifs shown below. Then cut each one out in fabric, leaving ⅜″ turnbacks. Snip the turnbacks as shown in the diagram opposite, top, so that the curves will lie flat when the shapes are sewn down.

Now assemble the patchwork quilt itself with a checkerboard of calico, gingham, and white fabrics. On each white square position any one of the animals, and stitch each in place, as in the diagram. Embroider all details, the flowers in lazy daisy stitch, the grass in

stem or fishbone, and all dots in French knots. Baste the quilt top, batting, and lining together. Now with running stitch and quilting thread, quilt around each motif with even running stitches. In the calico squares quilt a smiling sun, hearts, or similar suitable shapes. When the quilt is complete, lay a gathered eyelet ruffle facedown all around. Machine-stitch it in place, turn it back, and lightly hem the backing to it. Each square of the original quilt measures 7″, so a pillow made with four squares joined together, or a baby block made with six (see photo, page 114), would make an attractive set.

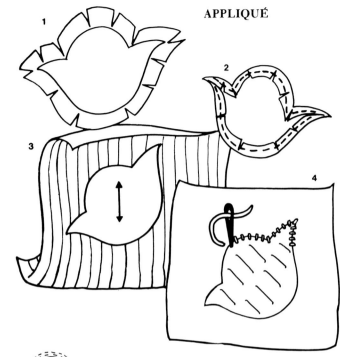

APPLIQUÉ

APPLIQUÉ DIAGRAM

1. Cut out shapes and snip turnbacks all around.
2. Press and baste shapes.
3. Pin them so that their grain lines are parallel to the background fabric.
4. Sew down with tiny stitches at right angles to the edge.

Shadow Quilting

THIS unusual form of quilting relies for its effect on transparent fabrics. Colored felt, wool, or cotton fabrics in separated shapes like a stencil are sandwiched between two layers of organdy, Dacron, batiste, or similar material, and held in place by running stitches all around the edges of each motif.

The pattern opposite (in color on page 41) can be used for a tray cloth or place mat as shown, or as a tablecloth with the design repeated in all four corners. It could also be used wherever a transparent effect is needed, such as in a lampshade or on window curtains. Instead of colors, white felt, wool, or fabric could be used to make beautiful "white on white" designs. Tape one layer of organdy on top and trace the design onto the organdy with a hard pencil. Then make tracing-paper patterns of the individual flowers and leaves. Cut them out in fabric and lay them in position on top of the organdy on the design. A tiny touch of Elmer's Glue-All may help to hold them in position. Now take up the organdy and baste a second layer on top, holding all the layers together with the basting stitch (shown on page 106). Finally, work all around the design with running stitches, using white quilting thread. A gingham ribbon was put in in the same way to border the tray cloth shown here, and the hems were turned in and blind-stitched together. (For blind stitching, see page 105.)

SHADOW QUILTING

GAMES FOR NEEDLEPLAY

Jack Card Table

THE knave of clubs in bargello stitches makes a cover for a folding card table that can be permanently attached to the table. Then you can hang it on the wall as a decorative panel when you are not using it for playing. The original, shown in color on page 44, was done on #12 canvas with three threads of Persian yarn, and measures 33″ square.

Begin by folding a 38″ piece in half and in half again. With a hard pencil, mark the creases, pulling the pencil lightly between the threads. Now you have a foundation for following the graph opposite. Start in the center and work the central square with four clubs in it (two are shown on the graph). Color changes and direction of stitch are shown by the different thicknesses of lines on the diagram. Once you have completed the central square, you can count out and mark the other sections with pencil on the canvas. All sections enclosed in bold outlines are worked in satin stitch. Work these first, fill in the bargello-patterned sections, and then outline with stem stitch wherever heavy lines are shown on the chart. Leave no spaces for these outlines—work the adjoining sections right into the same holes, then work the stem stitch on top of the previous stitching. Work the faces in brick stitch, the eyes in satin; then work the features right over the previous stitching. Note that on the graph the spade to the right of the jack is worked horizontally in double brick stitch, and the background is in horizontal random bargello.

Once one quarter-section is completed, turn the canvas and follow the graph again. This will mean that each background section will be at an opposite angle. The blue background outside the circle was done in laid work with long split stitches underneath, but you could use any one of your favorite stitches to contrast with the other stitching.

Backgammon Boards

The soft yet long-wearing surface of needlepoint is ideal for playing backgammon, and bargello stitches are a natural because the V-formation of the patterns can be fitted right into each point, as you see here. This board was done in teal blue, brown, navy, and cream, with an orange-red Gobelin stitch background, but you can of course work any patterns in any colors, as long as you alternate light and dark points.

The board in the photo measures 19″ x 24″ and was done on #10 canvas with three strands of Persian yarn. Begin by establishing the center of your canvas, and mark out the entire board with a pencil. First mark the rectangle enclosing the board—19″ x 24″. Then draw a 3″ wide vertical band from one side to the other. This forms the center panel and can be almost any width, according to the size of your men; but of course it must stretch right across. On either side of the center panel, mark out the areas for the base of each of the points. Each one is fifteen threads wide and two threads apart. To outline the points themselves, draw the vertical lines decreasing by one thread every twelve threads, as in the diagram. Notice that the uppermost block is nine threads deep with a single stitch projecting on top to form the tip.

To do the stitching, follow the bargello stitches shown in the graph. Begin with the first point at the left, A. This shows the first step of the light series of points, B shows the second step, and C shows the third. Complete each point before going to the next. Work the dark points (D, E, and F) in the same way. For the background and center panel, work Gobelin stitch over four threads of the canvas.

On pages 122 and 123 is the chart for a backgammon board with a skyscraper design, shown on page 43. It was done in shades of gray with black and white and a sunset background in reds, orange, and gold. The buildings may be worked with all kinds of slanting Gobelin stitches, and the background is effective worked in horizontal rows of stem stitch because the sunset coloring can be blended in stripes—shading out from dark to light. If you follow the pattern working on #12 canvas with all three threads of Persian yarn, your finished board will measure 14″ x 17″. Start in the center (marked by the arrow) and work out on either side. Leave about nine to twelve threads of space between the tops of skyscrapers on either side.

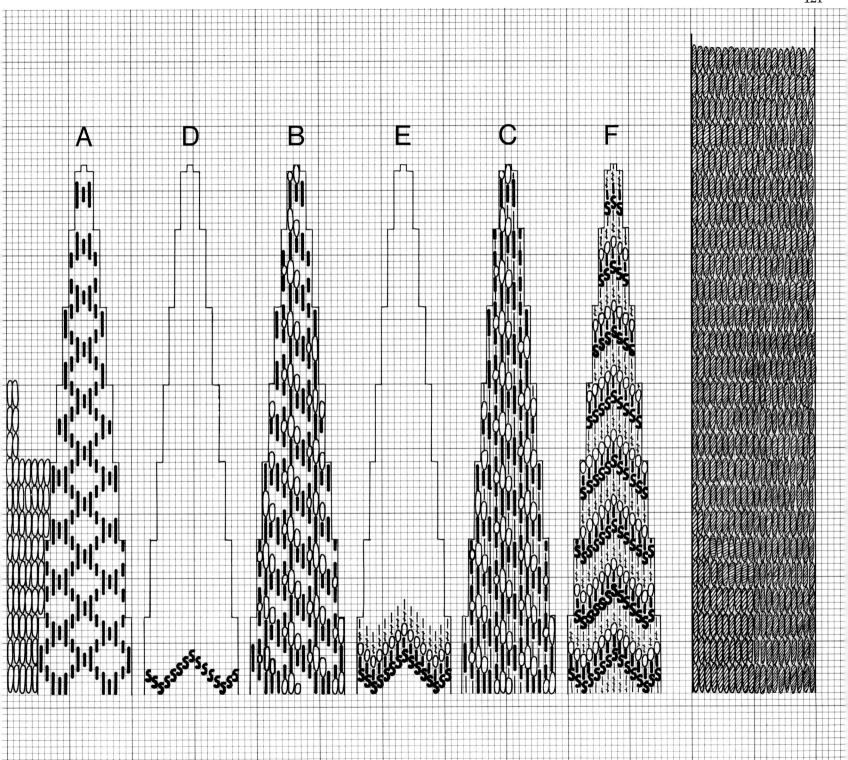

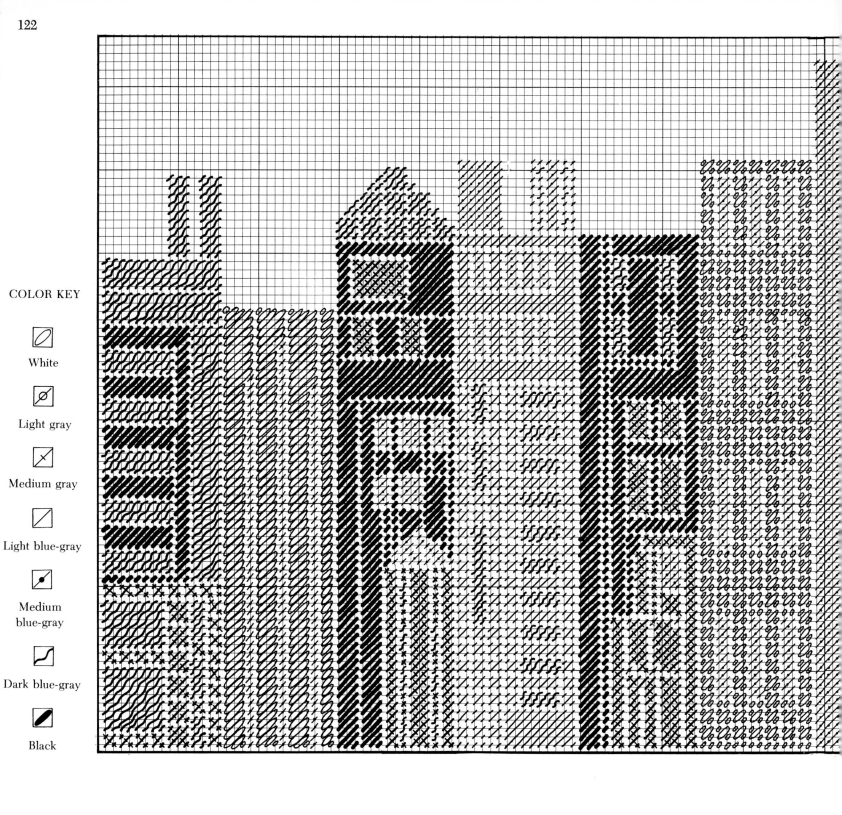

COLOR KEY

White

Light gray

Medium gray

Light blue-gray

Medium
blue-gray

Dark blue-gray

Black

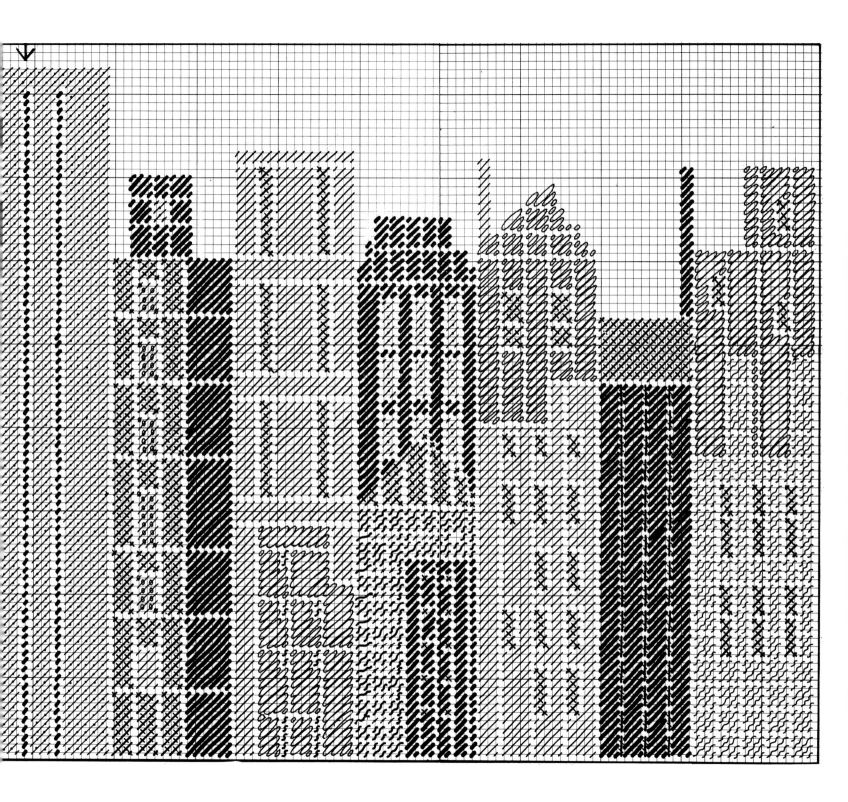

American Revolutionary Chessmen

YOU'LL find it amusing to make a chessboard with Revolutionary figures such as Martha and George Washington, George III and Queen Charlotte, Paul Revere as a knight on horseback, and Benjamin Franklin in place of a bishop. It's simple to count out the figures from the graphs on these pages, using red, white, and blue wools—of course—on interlocked canvas (which means that they can be cut close after working without fear of raveling). Count out the pieces on the canvas, leaving about ½″ between each piece. Do all stitching before cutting them out. Stitch the figures in tent stitch, with chain

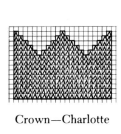

Crown—Charlotte

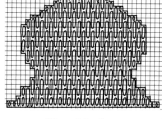

Hat—Martha

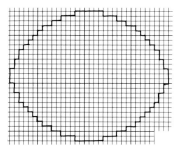

Bottom—Kings and Queens

Queen Charlotte   Martha Washington   Back—Charlotte Back—Martha

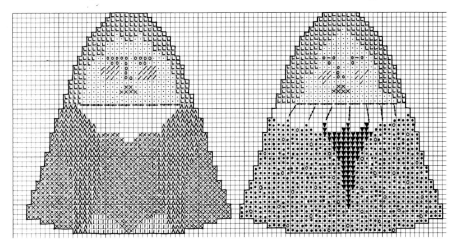

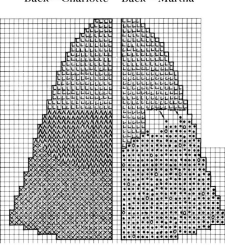

George Washington   King George   Back—King George   Back—George

stitch hair, brick stitch hats, split stitch horses' manes, and details such as ruffs and collars added on top afterward in French knots.

Each side will have sixteen men. Each man is made up of a front, back, bottom, and hat (front and back). Only half of each back is diagrammed, since it is symmetrical. When stitching, work each back as one piece, first counting it out as shown, then repeating exactly, counting out in the opposite direction of the center line.

Work one side of the horsemen facing left, as shown on the graph for "Knights." Then work the

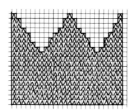

Crown—King George

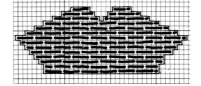

Hat—George

COLOR KEY

- ● Dark blue
- ▼ Dark brown
- L Light Gray
- ✕ Red
- O Beige
- ╱ Rose (pink)
- · Facial colors
- + Light brown
- ➤ Light Blue
- ▢ White
- ∧ Ocher
- 0 Off-white
- ➖ Black
- — Medium Gray
- S Medium Beige
- ≢ Sky blue

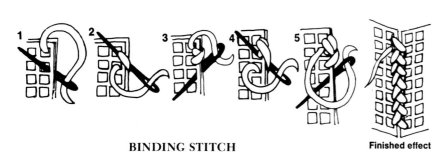

BINDING STITCH   **Finished effect**

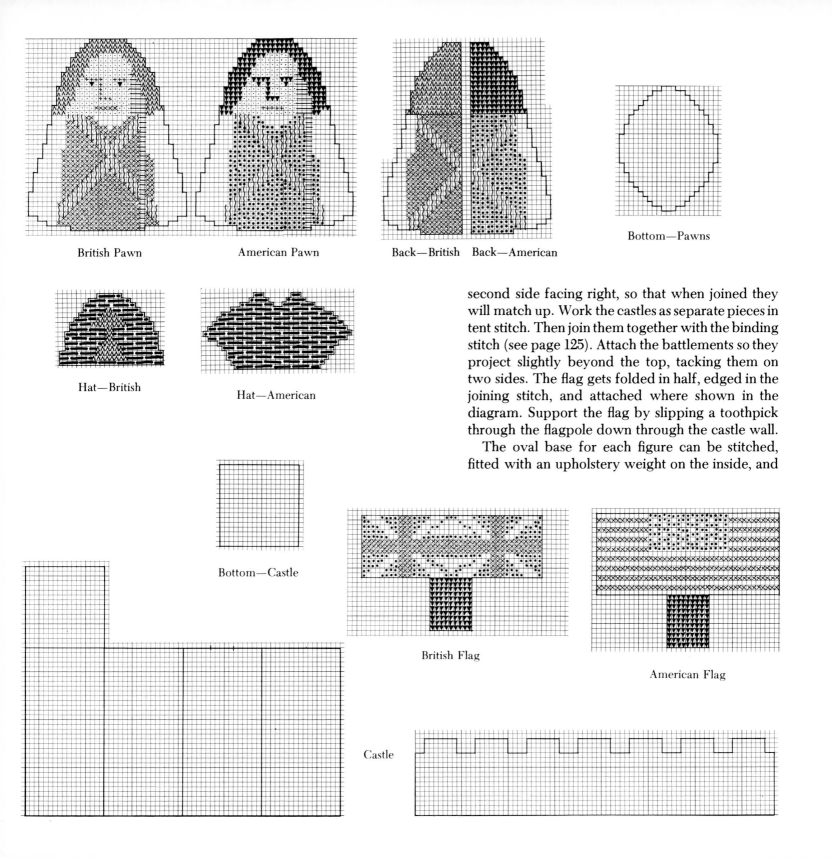

British Pawn

American Pawn

Back—British Back—American

Bottom—Pawns

Hat—British

Hat—American

second side facing right, so that when joined they will match up. Work the castles as separate pieces in tent stitch. Then join them together with the binding stitch (see page 125). Attach the battlements so they project slightly beyond the top, tacking them on two sides. The flag gets folded in half, edged in the joining stitch, and attached where shown in the diagram. Support the flag by slipping a toothpick through the flagpole down through the castle wall.

The oval base for each figure can be stitched, fitted with an upholstery weight on the inside, and

Bottom—Castle

British Flag

American Flag

Castle

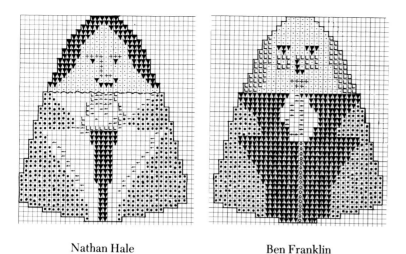

Nathan Hale   Ben Franklin

American Bishops

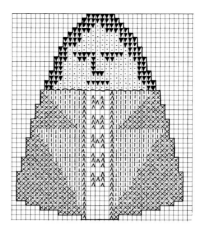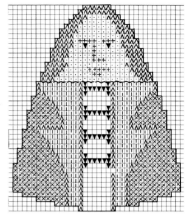

General Cornwallis   General Burgoyne

British Bishops

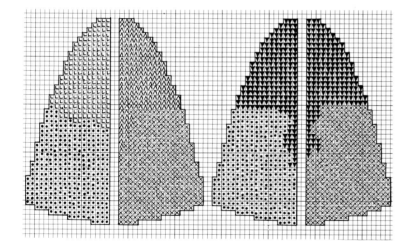

Back—Franklin   Back—Burgoyne   Back—Hale   Back—Cornwallis

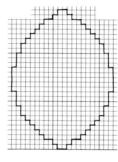

Bottom—Bishops

Hat—British Knight

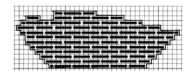

Hat—American Knight

then laced to the completed figures, which have
been filled with cotton. The chessboard itself can be
done in blue-and-white patchwork as shown, or
worked in needlepoint to coordinate with the chess-
men. The ideal size of each square of the board
is 2½″. The average height of the figures is 5″—
worked on #12 interlocked canvas—and slightly
larger if worked on #10 plastic canvas (the smallest
plastic mesh available).

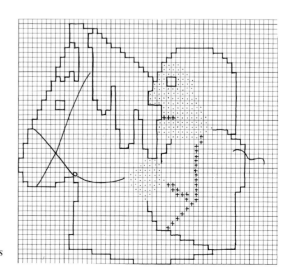

Knights

ONE-COLOR SPECTRUM

Black-and-gold Embroidery

WHEN you limit your palette to one color, you must use stitches to work for you, providing tone variations by contrasting solid areas with open lacy patterns. Black-and-gold embroidery, which originated in Spain, can provide inspiration for all kinds of geometric patterns done in one color.

Instead of using the traditional black with gold metal threads, in the shell design opposite I used shades of brown with gold silk, working on an evenweave linen. You could work on monk's cloth, Indian Head cotton, evenweave linen, or even needlepoint canvas, because each of these fabrics has a regular mesh that is essential for developing the geometric patterns. The scale of your stitches will depend on the fineness or boldness of the material you select—it's a good idea to collect samples of the various fabrics to experiment with and discover which size you prefer to work with.

To transfer the design opposite, trace half the central shell and fold it to make a mirror image and create an accurate complete shell. Then you can glue this paper pattern to thin cardboard or sandpaper and cut it out to make a firm template. When you realize that the shells fit together like a jigsaw puzzle, you will quickly see that you can fit shells above and below this first central one, arranging the upper curve of one to nestle into the lower edge of another, making an overall repeat pattern of any size.

Work in any one strong color, varying the thickness of the thread and the geometric patterns used for filling the spaces in order to give contrasting effects of light and dark. The narrow points are satin-stitched in cotton floss with French knots worked on top; above them the solid sections are worked closely in stripes of fishbone stitch. Then the geometric filling stitches are worked, alternating each horizontal row of shell shapes with solid or open lacy patterns.

On page 130 you will find a series of diagrams of stitches that can give filigree or bold effects if you vary the thickness of the floss you are using. Always work these stitches with a blunt tapestry needle so that you slip between the threads of the material and do not split through them.

Scherensnitte

A COMPLETELY different approach is the "Scherensnitte," or cut-paper design, shown on page 131. This Swiss folk art with its silhouette shapes is ideal for blackwork designs. By making a sampler of the stitches shown on page 130 you can decide which ones best fit your shapes before you begin. As you see, the stitches are based on either cross stitch or back stitch. You will find it easy to count them out from the graph if you first stretch the design in an embroidery frame.

Always start in the center of each shape to establish your pattern; then fill in the places where the pattern may have been interrupted by the edge of the design later on. The effectiveness of the whole thing relies on contrasts—solid bold areas against light filigree patterns, with perhaps a touch of gold metal thread here and there to make it lively. Instead of black and gold, you could try green and gold—or blue and silver. Any one color is fine, as long as it is a strong enough contrast with your background linen.

Needleweaving

DARNING patterns, woven in with a blunt needle on evenweave linen, are very similar to blackwork stitches, and in fact are sometimes combined with them in a design in which close, solid fillings are needed to contrast with more open ones. I made the border (left) for a set of place mats for my Nantucket house, working entirely in darning stitch on deep blue linen with white cotton floss.

It is best to work this sort of design out on graph paper first; then you can make alterations with an eraser instead of a pair of scissors—which is much more satisfactory. Once you have your design outlined on the graph (there is no need to draw out all the patterned fillings; you can put those in as you go along), you can mount the fabric in an embroidery frame, and with a blunt needle start weaving. In this design, it is easiest to establish your pattern by starting with the bottom border, going over five threads, picking up one, over five, under one, and so on for the whole length of the row. Then return, weaving the next row immediately above the first. The trees, house, and windmill can be woven individually in horizontal rows, counting them from the photo. Notice that the roof is woven vertically for contrast.

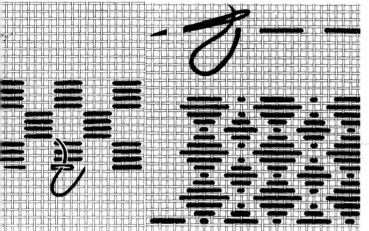

DARNING STITCHES

Darning patterns are built up by weaving under and over the background fabric, row by row, as shown.

Meissen "Blue Onion" Pattern

THE familiar Meissen china pattern is a design that looks beautiful in shades of one color—any color. Blue is the traditional one, but you could make a coordinating set—wastepaper basket, tissue box, and hand towels to go with your bathroom—using terra-cotta, green, brown, gold, or even black on white—or work with white on any contrasting color background. For hand towels, the ideal method of transferring the pattern is with Stitch Witchery or Wonder Under —that fusible Pellon web which allows you to sew right through, then tear it away afterward. Anyone who has tried to stitch on the deep pile of a towel knows how difficult it is. The stitches sink

Wastepaper basket with Meissen "Blue Onion" pattern in crewel. Hand towels with the same design, in cotton floss for easy washing.

between the pile and look ratty. With the Pellon web overlay, the stitches stay smoothly on top of the pile, with raised, crisp outlines. It is important to find the lightest weight in adhesive Pellon; this is the kind that tears away like a cobweb around the design after the stitching is complete.

Begin by tracing the design onto the Stitch Witchery with a permanent marker (right). Mount the whole thing into an embroidery frame and baste the Pellon in position, as in the photo. Work with simple crewel stitches, using wool or cotton floss—in buttonhole, chain, stem, and padded satin stitches—varying the shades of blue, as in the photo on page 48. When the stitching is finished, tear away the web, rubbing with the flat points of the scissors to remove unwanted bits and pieces. Your design will be perfectly neat, with the edges sitting on top of the pile as if by magic —and no one will know your secret!

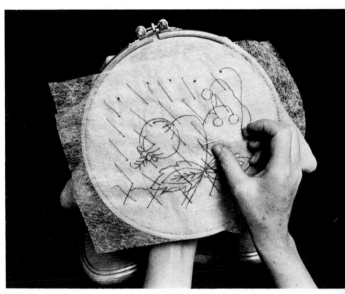

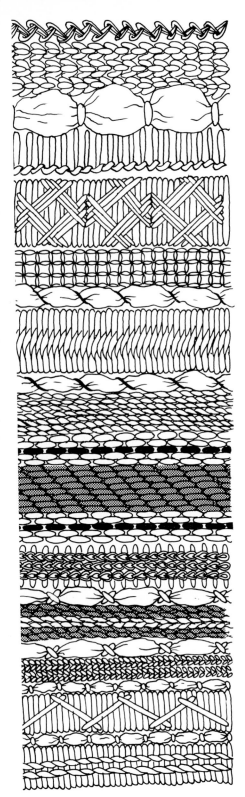

ZIGZAG CHAIN

RAISED CHAIN

PUFFY COUCHING

BUTTONHOLE

GOBELIN STITCH with open
Waffle Stitch worked on top

FAGGOT STITCH

PUFFY COUCHING

ROUMANIAN

PUFFY COUCHING

STEM STITCH

CABLE STITCH with Back Stitch
worked between rows

GOBELIN

CABLE STITCH with Back Stitch
worked between rows

RAISED CHAIN STITCH

PUFFY COUCHING

RAISED STEM STITCH

PUFFY COUCHING

REVERSE TENT
PUFFY COUCHING

GOBELIN STITCH with
Herringbone Stitch worked on top

PUFFY COUCHING

GOBELIN STITCH with
Stem Stitch worked on top

Textured Stripes

FROM flat, lacy blackwork to darning to one-color crewel, we go to the bold texture of stripes done in needlepoint and crewel on canvas. The pillows shown on page 47 could of course be done in combinations of many colors, but because of their many different stitches the design has more impact if shades of only one color are used. The originals were worked in browns, ranging from almost black, all the way to creamy white; but you could choose shades of any of the "naturals"—rust, indigo, chestnut, caramel—or work in all white for a lovely subtle effect.

Once you have decided which color you are going to use, start collecting threads in as many different varieties as you can find. These will be your working "palette," as it were—ranging from fine cotton floss or shiny crochet cotton to thick, creamy roving, unspun wool with a soft, fluffy look. Wools for knitting and weaving are so exciting you may find it hard to choose, but you can let yourself go with texture since your color scheme is limited.

Most versatile of the stitches is perhaps couching. You can couch anything from roving to ribbons to bold bundles of wool or fine cotton or silks. Pulled work and openwork stitches (see page 161) provide great contrasts, and the basic tent stitch (continental or basket weave) is sometimes a restful background for the more raised stitches worked in heavy threads.

Crewel stitches such as couching, chain, and herringbone; pulled work, such as faggot stitch; and needlepoint stitches, such as reverse tent—all have been used interchangeably in this design. They may be found by referring to the Stitch Index on page 192.

Wing Chair

CREWEL is traditionally done in many colors with fine crewel wools, but it is an interesting departure to work with shades of one color, using three strands of Persian wool for a bold contemporary effect. As you see from the color photo on page 50, my chair was worked in shades of brown, but since a great deal of the design is done with open patterns contrasted by solid fillings, the "Tree of Life" design could also be beautiful worked predominantly in white on brown linen. You can enlarge (see page 176) and repeat the line drawing opposite (the bottom fits on the top to form a continuously growing tree) for curtains, a wing chair, a bedspread, or a room divider; or you could take only the central part of the design to make a tote bag or a chair seat. Instructions for the traditional crewel stitches used may be found on pages 182 to 185. You can make your own combinations, such as close herringbone outlined with stem stitch for the main stems, and chain stitch for the smaller stems; laid work tied with cross bars for the large central flower, with open fishbone stitch for lower leaves and close buttonhole for the upper sections. You could work the bird's wings in buttonhole stitch with close herringbone for his tail. Whichever stitches you choose, fill in all the main areas of the design first; then outline and add accents, such as French knots, on top afterward.

3-D COLLAGE

Free-standing Needlepoint Appliqué

THE skirt of the Elizabethan lady, counterpart of the eighteenth-century box on page 54, is worked in petitpoint, then gathered and applied to the fabric to look like a real skirt. It is attached on the sides and top only; the bottom is hemmed back and left loose so that it stands out in relief. You can apply the needlepoint by taking turnbacks, basting them back, and stitching the appliqué needlepoint down with tiny invisible stitches. Alternatively, you could hold the two sides of the skirt firm, as shown in the diagram. This method takes longer but makes

the fabrics become as one, so the appliqué will stay in place forever. The other stitches used in the design are trellis stitch (sleeves, bird, and tree trunks), satin stitch (bodice), gathered net (ruffs and cuffs), French knots (coif), looped stem stitch (grass), padded satin (leaves), and raised cup stitch (fruits). (See pages 182 to 191.)

This graph is based on the colors shown in the illustration at the top of color page 54, but any color combinations may be used.

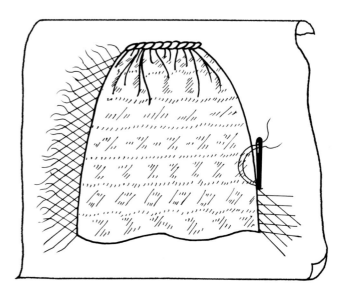

To apply the needlepoint, ravel out the threads, one by one, around the edges of the finished work. Thread a needle, take them through to the back; then knot them together on the reverse side to hold them firmly. Trim ends.

The skirt is worked on the diagonal of the canvas. Begin with the black line at the bottom and work fifty stitches across. Then work one row of background color next to the black.

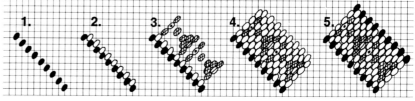

1. Stitch black outline.

2. Stitch first row of background color.

3. Stitch pattern.

4. Fill in background.

5. Finished section.

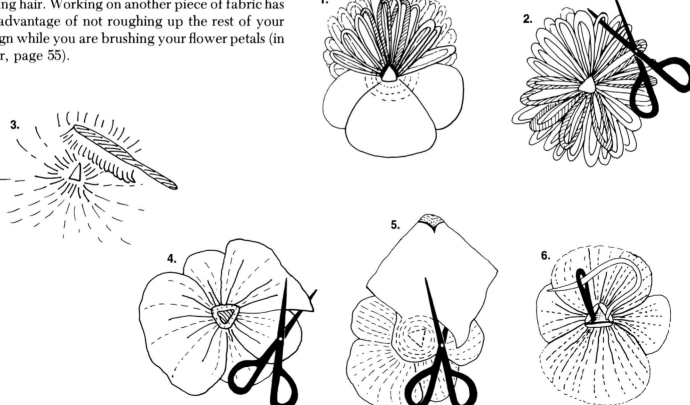

Brushed-wool Pansies

You could make almost any three-dimensional flowers in brushed-wool stitch, but pansies—because of their flat, velvety petals—are perhaps the most ideal. You will find the pansies easy to do if you work them on a separate piece of fabric, then cut them out and apply them. This means you can work the flat parts of your crewel design first, then work, clip, brush, and shape your pansies separately and arrange them just like a flower arrangement on the fabric. You can stitch them in place when you are satisfied with their correct size, position, and color scheme. The brushing is best done with a "teasel" brush—a little wire-toothed circle you can buy in a craft store. Or use a brush for teasing hair. Working on another piece of fabric has the advantage of not roughing up the rest of your design while you are brushing your flower petals (in color, page 55).

1. *Making the Loops:* Follow turkey work, page 190. Shaded loops indicate accent colors, which should be added in final rows nearest center of pansy.
2. *Snipping the Loops*
3. *Brushing the Cut Loops*
4. *Trimming the Loops* (following the shape of the petals printed on the fabric): Cut some of the accent colors slightly shorter, following the color photograph (page 55). Brush and trim alternately until a silky effect of blended colors has been obtained. Work center of pansy with satin stitch and bullion knots.
5. *Cutting Away Fabric on Reverse Side*
6. *Stitching Finished Pansy into Position:* First pin all the pansies in place, establishing the correct angle for each one. Then, using the same color thread, take a few satin stitches (at the same angle as the previous ones) across the center, to secure the pansy invisibly.

Raised Bouquet

THIS bouquet (in color on page 54) is a potpourri of raised flowers, done in raised cup stitch, raised needleweaving, brushed-wool stitch, and free-standing "pipe cleaner" petals. In contrast, the flat pansies and daisies at the base are done in long and short, lazy daisy stitch, and French knots, with open fishbone-stitch leaves forming a lacy background. (See pages 182 to 191.) The whole bouquet is then tied with a real velvet ribbon lightly tacked in place.

1. To make the pipe-cleaner flowers, bend a pipe cleaner as shown (right) to make three petals at a time.
2. Then, using a blunt needle, weave back and forth to completely cover your pipe-cleaner base.
3. Since you are working "in the air," as it were, you must secure your starting thread by holding it under the weaving, as at 2 and 3.
4. Push in as many rows as you can close together to make a solid petal. End off by running the thread up into the previous weaving and begin each new thread in the same way as before (diagrams 2 and 3).
5. When you have enough sets of three completed to make a circle of petals, bend them to curve around the center of the daisy and attach them to the design by stitching them down firmly at the bend between each petal. These small stitches can then be covered by rings of French knots, forming the center of the flower. The petals can then be curved at any angle to form the effect you want.

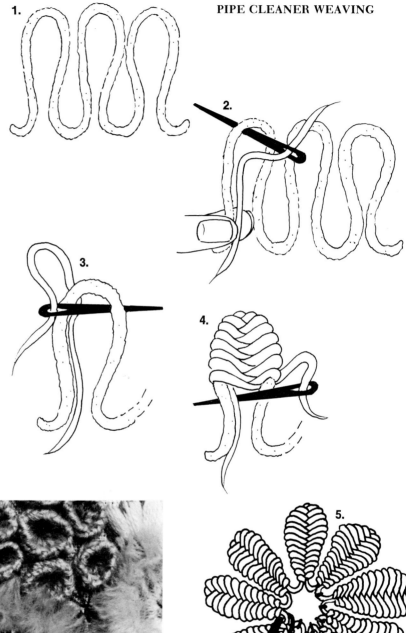

Three Dimensions in Soft Sculpture

ONCE you start working with fabrics and take off into the realms of soft sculpture, there'll be no limit to your creativity. The models close at hand (forgive the pun), all ready for you to sculpt them in stitches, are your hands and face. Simply trace around your hands, allow half an inch or more for padding (things always become much smaller when they are "in the round"), stitch two pieces of fabric together, right sides facing, then turn them inside out, pad them, and stitch them to a belt, as in my "Hawaiian Snowflake" quilted dress (left). Or use a smaller pair of padded hands on a picture, holding a spray of raised flowers. Or, for a great "conversation" dress, have lots of hands appearing out of pockets all over an evening skirt. To make your hands shapely, you should work with soft materials such as muslin or Dacron/cotton combinations, and pad with resilient batting such as lamb's wool or Mountain Mist polyester, which won't go into lumps. The same is true for "faces." It is easier to make a pattern first, so that you can realize your final face in high relief. Begin by drawing a face in profile on a double layer of fabric. Baste with small stitches, seam and snip the turnbacks so that the curves will lie smooth. Open it up, round it if necessary with a dart under the nose and chin, and pad the nose and chin first, then the whole face. Now, with a felt marker, you will be able to position the features exactly where you want them.

Add brushed-wool or turkey-work hair, quilted wings, or any other details that will just add finishing touches.

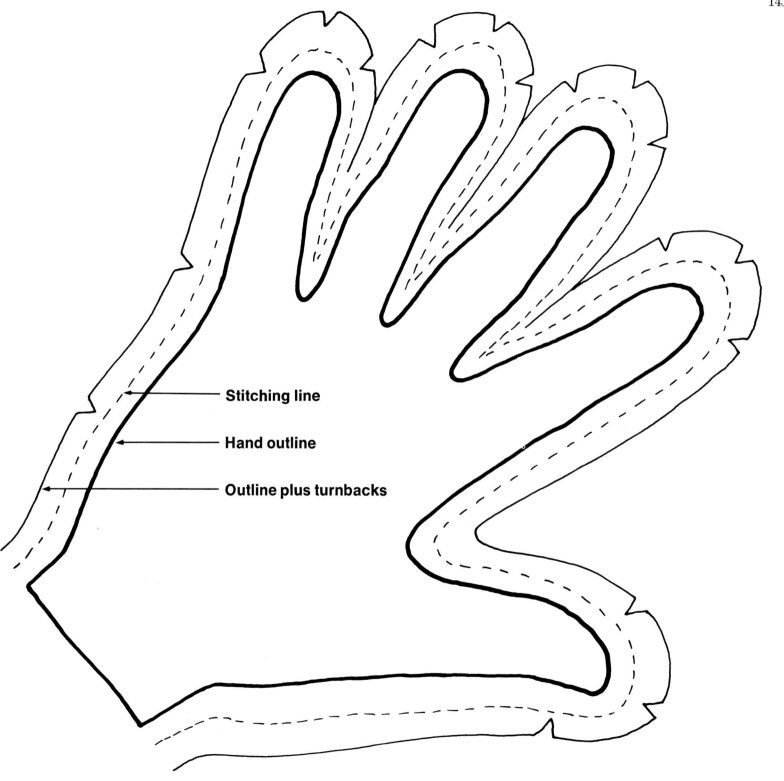

Stitching line

Hand outline

Outline plus turnbacks

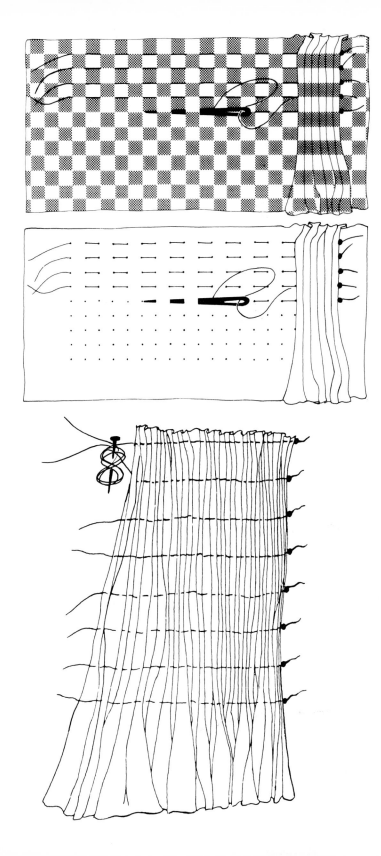

FUN AND FASHION

Smocking

SMOCKING is coming back into fashion, with all sorts of exciting possibilities. You can make blouses, baby dresses, nightdresses—even a wedding dress! Or you can smock smaller things, such as a pair of mules, a drawstring bag, lampshades, aprons—anything that has decorative, elastic gathers is suitable for this traditionally English form of needlework.

Since smocking is a way of holding folds in fabric, any sort of material lightweight enough to gather well may be used. Choose printed cotton, dotted Swiss, wool challis, or—easiest to begin on —striped cotton or checked gingham. Always allow three times the amount of fabric for gathering; in other words, the finished smocked area will end up one-third the size you started with.

Before the garment can be made up, the smocking must be done, and before the smocking can be done, the fabric must be evenly gathered. Either use gingham fabric to follow as a guide, or iron a smocking spot transfer pattern (available at some needlework stores) to the reverse side of your material. Begin each row with a knot and a back stitch for strength, and always have enough thread in your needle to complete each line. On the gingham, come up on one side of the square, go down at the other. With the spots, come up on one and go down on the next. Work each row immediately following the previous one so that, when drawn up, the gathers form even, continuous folds—called "reeds"—side by side. Draw them up and secure them by wrapping them around pins for easy adjustment while the smocking is being done.

Work the stitches on the right side on the surface of the folds, following the diagrams on pages 146 and 147. Use cotton floss and start with a knot that may be buried in the first fold on the reverse side. When complete, draw out the gathering threads and hold the smocking in the steam formed by throwing a cloth over the up-ended iron. This will raise the stitches and "set" the gathers at whatever size you want them to be.

The baby dress shown here and in color on page 58 has a very deep circular necklace of smocking all around the top. The pattern for it is shown below, and the same one may be used for a dress or blouse of any size, with long or short sleeves, by making simple adjustments. Following the graph, if you make every square equal 1″, you will end up with a baby dress approximately 8″ across the yoke, with a 7″ sleeve (measured from the neck), and 15″ from top to bottom (not including a hem, which should be approximately 5″). When cutting out the pattern,

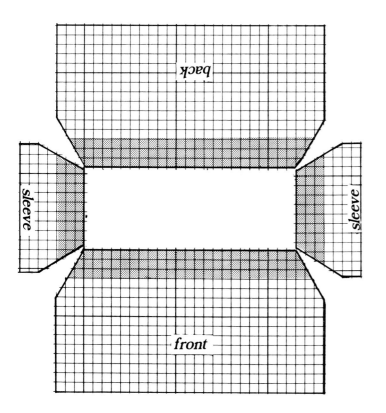

leave ⅜″ seam allowance all around. First, hem the sleeve; next, join the shoulder seams. Then iron on the smocking spots (in the area shaded on the pattern) and gather all around the circular top (as described before). Smock, as you have gathered, in one continuous piece. The pattern can easily be enlarged or reduced proportionately. To make the same pattern into an average-size adult dress, make each square measure 2″ instead of 1″.

STEM, OR
OUTLINE, STITCH

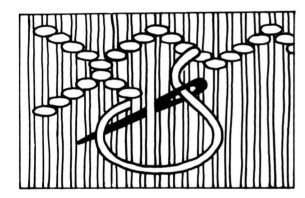

CABLE STITCH

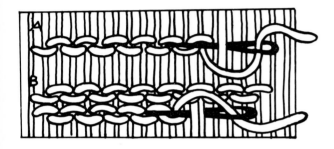

CHEVRON STITCH

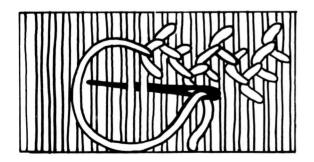

FEATHER STITCH

SMOCKING STITCHES

STEM, OR OUTLINE

This is a good basic stitch to begin with, as both cable and chevron (shown below) are based on it. Stem stitch is excellent for controlling the gathers at the top of a band of smocking close to where it fits into a yoke or band of fabric. Begin with a knot, come up on the left side of the first reed on the left. With the thread above the needle, take a shallow stitch into the next reed, with the needle slanting slightly downward, as shown. Alternatively the thread may be kept below with the needle slanting upward, as long as it is kept either above or below for the whole length of the line.

CABLE

Cable is exactly like outline stitch, except that with each stitch the thread is held alternately above or below the needle. If the first row was begun with the thread below the needle, begin the second row with the thread above so that the two stitches fit right next to each other, making the effect of a cable, as in the diagram.

CHEVRON

This is one of the most versatile stitches, good for the focal point of a band of smocking. It can be worked in many different ways. Begin on the left and, holding the needle horizontally, work four stitches (one on each reed) with the thread above the needle. Take each succeeding stitch slightly below the previous one. On the fifth stitch, hold the thread *below* the needle, then start working up again. At the top of this row, start working up again. At the top of this row, start again with the thread above the needle, and descend again, as in the diagram. In other words, at the top of the chevron the last stitch becomes number one of the descending line. At the bottom of this line the last stitch will become number one of the next upward line, and so on. *All chevrons are worked in this way.*

FEATHER

This is an open lacy stitch with great possibilities for variations. It may be worked in straight rows, or in chevrons, just like diamond lattice. Begin on the right. Come up, take the first two folds together with the thread held under the needle, as in the diagram. Move down and take the second and third folds in the same way, with the thread under the needle. Then take the third and fourth together. Loop the thread under the needle in the other direction and work upward, repeating the first three steps in the other direction. Continue going up for three stitches and down for three, to form a chevron pattern.

DIAMOND LATTICE

This is a very useful light lattice pattern for covering wide areas. Start at the left. Come up on the left of the first reed, take a stitch level into the right side of the second reed, with the thread below the needle. Now come up on the left side of the second reed, and take a stitch into the third reed with the thread below the needle. Then take a stitch into the fourth reed level with the thread above the needle. Continue, following the diagram. The diamond stitch may be worked in rows exactly repeating each other, leaving a space the depth of one stitch between each row, or each row may be reversed to form the lattice, as shown in the diagram.

SPOT HONEYCOMB

This stitch is the most elastic of the smocking stitches; and to show it off properly it should be stretched out to its full width before setting it into a garment. Start at the left and take one stitch over the first two reeds together. Then take a second stitch, but slide the needle right through the reed, as in the diagram. Come out slightly to the left and above on the right-hand reed of the pair. Then take a stitch over this and the next reed together, but slide the needle *down* to come out slightly to the left of the reed, on a level with the first stitch taken. Continue wrapping pairs of reeds together along the row. Care must be taken to make the two stitches come up and go down in the same hole so they appear to be one. On the next row, take one reed from the first pair, and one from the second. Wrap these together to form a honeycomb effect.

VANDYKE

This stitch gives a very strong horizontal stripe since the stitching is quite solid and close. Start on the *right*, and take a stitch over the first two reeds together, as in the spot honeycomb. Now go up and *wrap* the third with the fourth, as in the diagram, to the end of the row. The thread passing from one "wrapping" to the next lies over the reeds instead of being concealed inside them as in spot honeycomb, giving a more "stitched" effect. Work the rows under each other with a space the depth of one stitch between each row. Either repeat the previous stitches exactly, or "split" the pairs of reeds as in spot honeycomb to make a lattice effect as before.

DIAMOND LATTICE STITCH

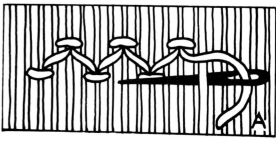
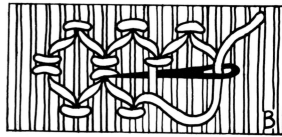

SPOT HONEYCOMB

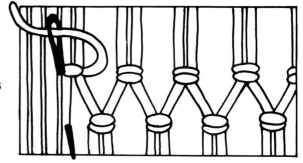

VANDYKE

Blue Jeans and Skirt

BECAUSE I wanted to add a touch of color to my blue jeans, I used all six strands of cotton floss for a bold effect, working the leaves in close herringbone stitch and the flowers in satin, straight, and stem stitches. I found it easier to open a seam all up one side of the leg so that I could work in a frame. I did the same thing in my natural linen skirt, adding rust, teal blue, beige, and brown to the patch pockets and using the same stitches as for the blue jeans.

If your are making your own clothing, always first pin your paper pattern together, try the garment on, and decide exactly where you want your embroidery to be. Then you could enlarge and transfer either design shown here, as I did; or rearrange them to form a "necklace" for around the top of a sweater; or for a completely different effect—work with three strands of cotton on a chiffon blouse.

The instructions for transferring designs to different materials are on page 177.

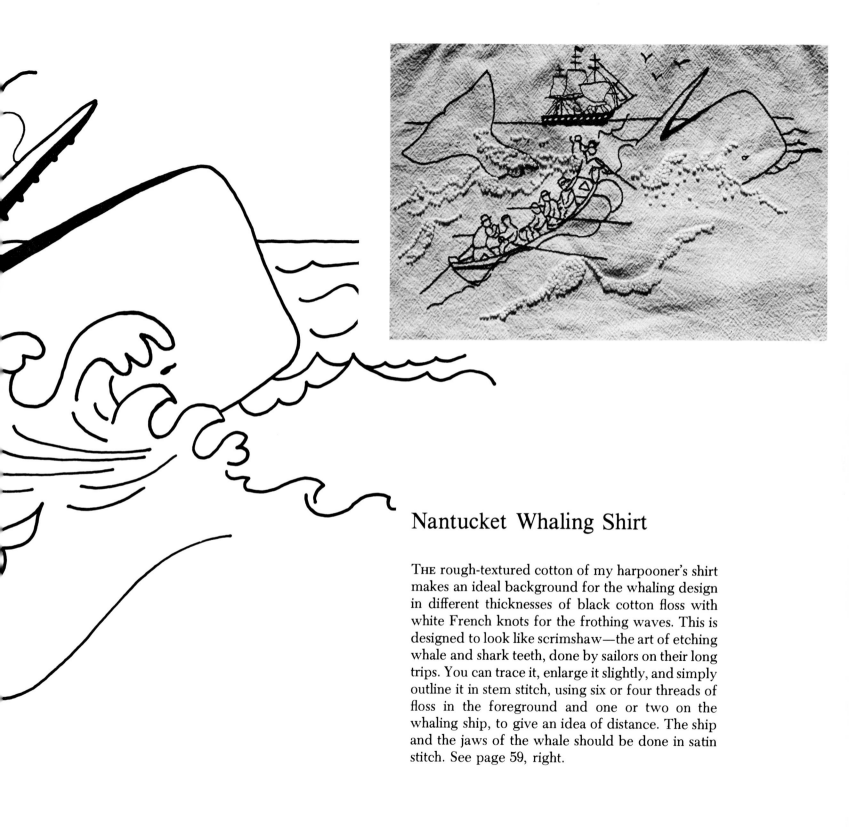

Nantucket Whaling Shirt

THE rough-textured cotton of my harpooner's shirt makes an ideal background for the whaling design in different thicknesses of black cotton floss with white French knots for the frothing waves. This is designed to look like scrimshaw—the art of etching whale and shark teeth, done by sailors on their long trips. You can trace it, enlarge it slightly, and simply outline it in stem stitch, using six or four threads of floss in the foreground and one or two on the whaling ship, to give an idea of distance. The ship and the jaws of the whale should be done in satin stitch. See page 59, right.

FROM THE GARDEN

Crewel Vegetables

VEGETABLES are wonderful subjects for needlework because they seem perfectly suited for different stitches—French knots for broccoli, padded satin for cherry tomatoes, split stitch for mushrooms, spider's webs for cauliflower, coral stitch for parsley, and so on. The vegetables shown here could be traced life-size, worked, and mounted, and used as a recipe file or a place to keep your shopping lists and other important memoranda, which always seem to accumulate untidily in the kitchen.

Other ways of using the vegetables would be to trace them onto needlepoint canvas to use as coasters, or transfer them to squares of plastic canvas and join them to make a great tote bag, or work them in squares in either needlepoint or crewel and join them like tiles to make a panel for the kitchen or dining room.

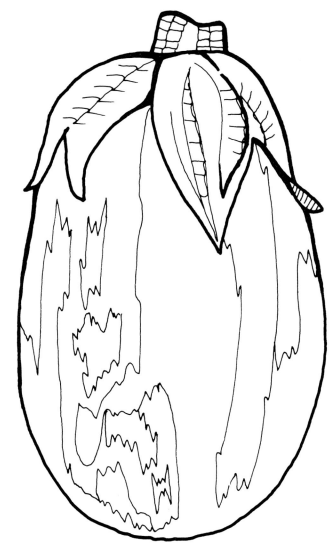

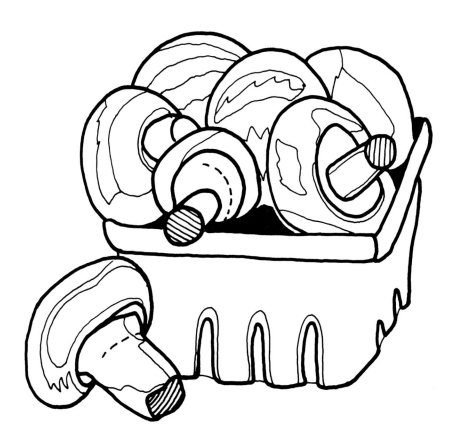

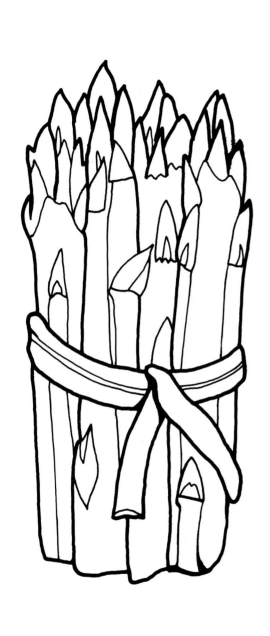

Field of Flowers in Crewel

CLOUDS of color (page 62) in bold Persian wool give this carpet of flower faces its excitement. You must scatter your colors in drifts and use bold textures, mixing all kinds of different wools if you like. You can trace the life-size design opposite (a quarter of a 12″ pillow is shown), turn it, and repeat it to keep the leaves on the outer border. Working on canvas or coarse linen, you can completely cover any surface—a garden chair, a kitchen stool, pillows, a bench, or even a rug—with this long-wearing needlework. Using six strands of Persian wool, work the stitches into one central hole in each flower. The stitch used is straight stitch, one of the simplest there is—just come up on the outline of the flower and go down into the center hole. Sometimes a few shorter stitches that do not go into the center may be needed to make a close overall covering at the edge and avoid crowding in the middle. Vary the length of the stitches to give the effect of petals, and make sure no open spaces of linen or canvas show between them.

The "French twist" in the center of each blossom is a combination French knot and bullion knot, but it has a much rougher look than either—which fits with the free, contemporary design. Work the French twists when all stitching is completed, following the instructions below:

FRENCH TWIST

1. With the fabric stretched in a frame, come up through the center of a flower.
2. Holding the thread tightly, twist the needle and thread between thumb and forefinger until "kinks" begin to appear in it.
3. Holding it tightly, with the left hand close to the fabric, with the right hand return the needle through the same hole, pulling lightly to form a twisted knot on the surface of the fabric.

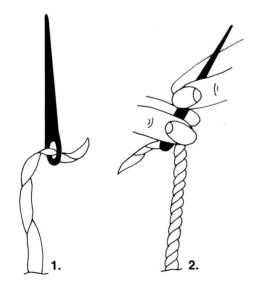

1. **2.**

3.

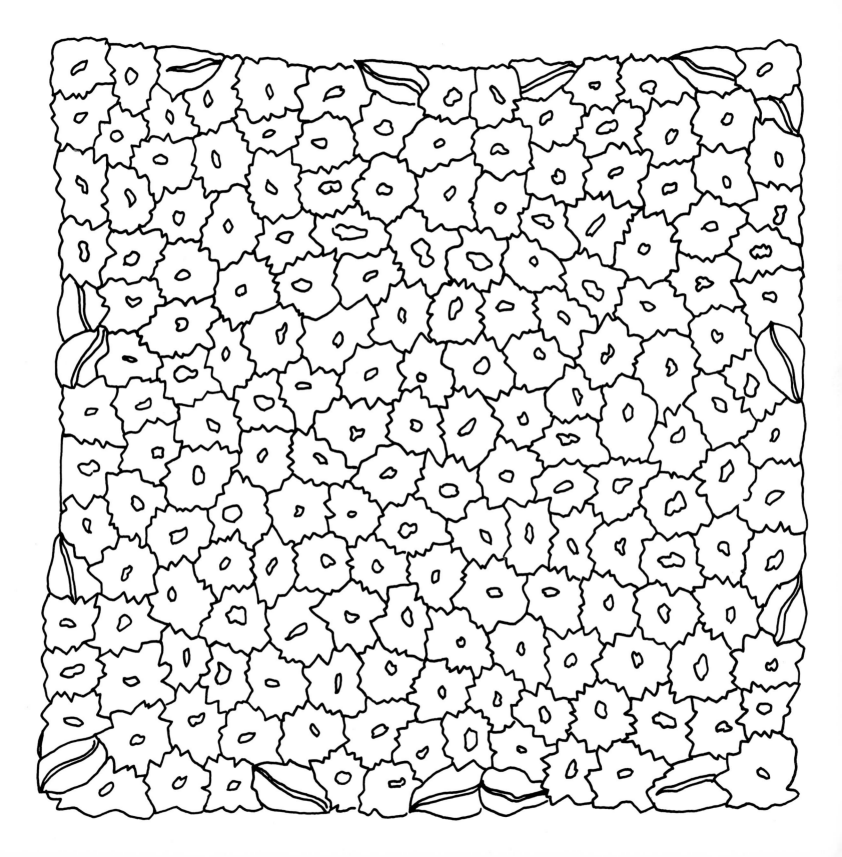

KALEIDOSCOPE BARGELLO

EACH of the patterns on pages 157 to 159 measures 16″ x 16″, and one-quarter of the full-size design is given. You could set them under glass to make table tops, use them as colorful pillows, or enlarge and join several to make a rug.

To make any one of the patterns, begin by finding the center of a 20″ square of #12 canvas. Do this by folding the canvas in half and in half again. Crease the folds firmly. Open it up and mark these center lines horizontally and vertically with a pencil. You can run the pencil lightly *between* the threads of the canvas, allowing them to guide you in keeping the lines straight. Stay in the groove *between* threads; do not mark lines on *top* of the threads of the canvas. To mark the diagonals, place the square of canvas flat on the table with one of the corners toward you. Kneel so that you are at eye level with it. Shift the canvas a little until you can see the clear ridges formed by the mesh, running diagonally across the canvas. Place a ruler beside the ridge you need to mark, and draw the line with a pencil. It is easier to mark lines with a pencil first— it can be erased if you make a mistake, and the firm point stays in the groove between the threads, keeping your lines precise. If necessary, darken the lines with a permanent marker.

Once you have prepared your canvas for kaleidoscope bargello, you can decide which type of design you would like to work. You have a choice of either the flame stitch geometric like the one on pages 64 and 65, where your stitches form the pattern, or the more graphic kind, where you outline your design and fill silhouette shapes with bargello or brick stitch patterns. On page 67 is one of these— the pink hibiscus, which is simply worked in satin stitch on the canvas, departing from the patterned effect of bargello altogether. Others are on the following pages and a variety are shown in color on page 66. To transfer them, just lay your prepared canvas over one-quarter, trace it, and repeat it exactly on the other three sides. Tape your design flat; maneuver the canvas so that it lies square on top (some pulling may be necessary to align the canvas with the lines of the pattern). Use a waterproof marker to trace curved lines and a pencil (which will stay between the lines of the canvas) to keep straight lines straight. Follow the stitches and colors shown on the graph and page 66, using three strands of Persian wool on the #12 canvas, or choose your own. Once you grow bold, you will find you can easily invent them as you go along.

To do any flame stitch geometric pattern (like the one formed with mirrors on page 66) you should begin on any of the four *straight* lines marked on your canvas (not diagonals). Work in bargello stitch (page 187) and count the main color out to form a "skeleton" all across this quarter of the canvas, working from the center line out to the diagonals on either side. Once the pattern is established in this way, you can repeat it on the other three sides. It is an easy matter to finally fill in with all the other colors. Notice in the photograph on pages 64 and 65 how the stitches share the same holes at the diagonals, and make the necessary adjustments to the pattern so that a clear diagonal line is formed like a "parting."

COLOR KEY	
White	1
Light brown	2
Orange	3
Purple	4
Red	5
Dark brown	6

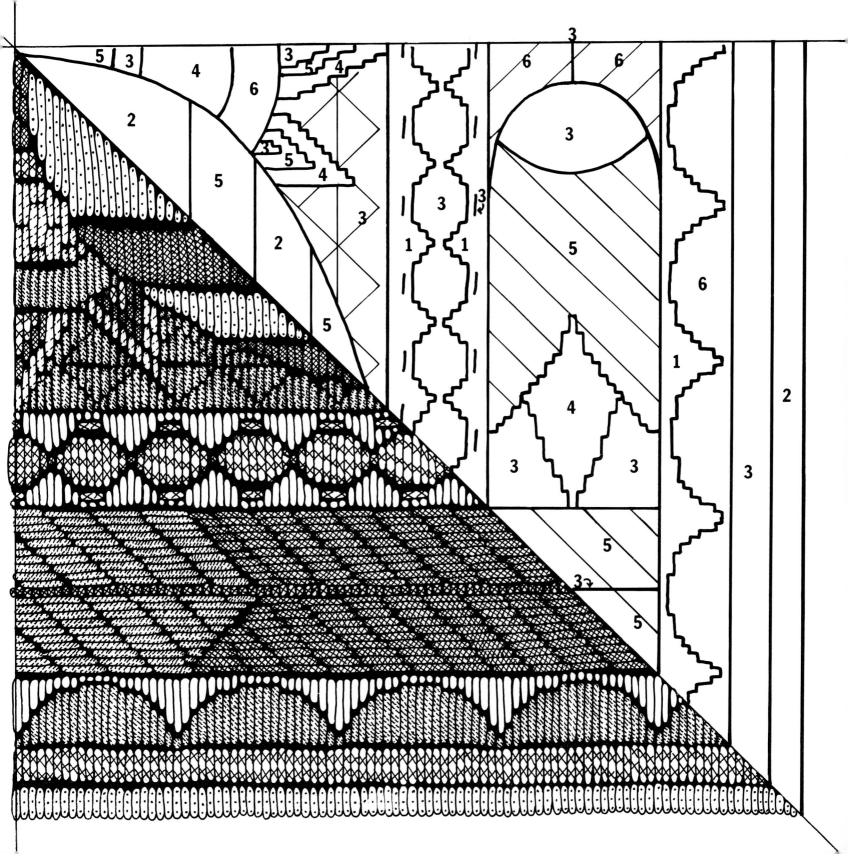

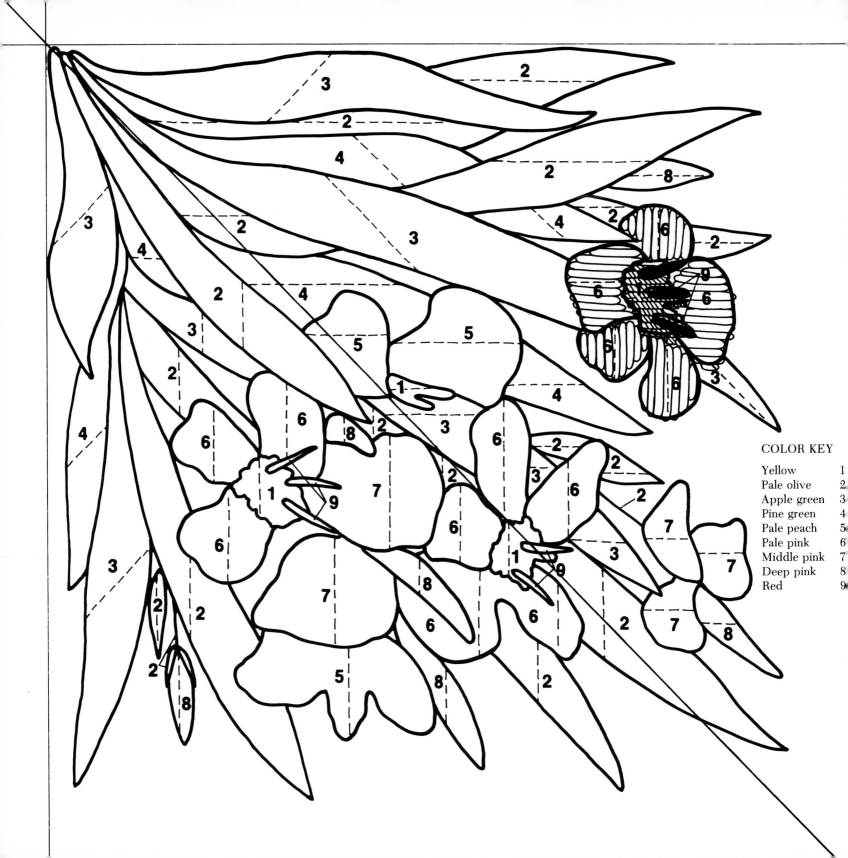

COLOR KEY

Yellow	1
Pale olive	2
Apple green	3
Pine green	4
Pale peach	5
Pale pink	6
Middle pink	7
Deep pink	8
Red	9

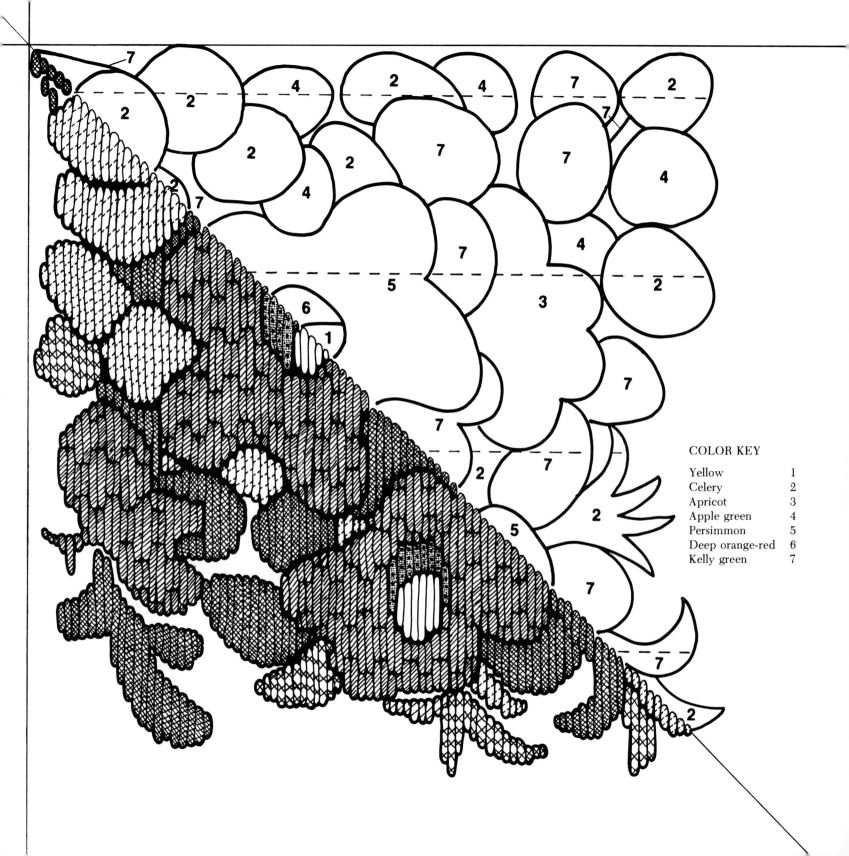

COLOR KEY

Color	
Yellow	1
Celery	2
Apricot	3
Apple green	4
Persimmon	5
Deep orange-red	6
Kelly green	7

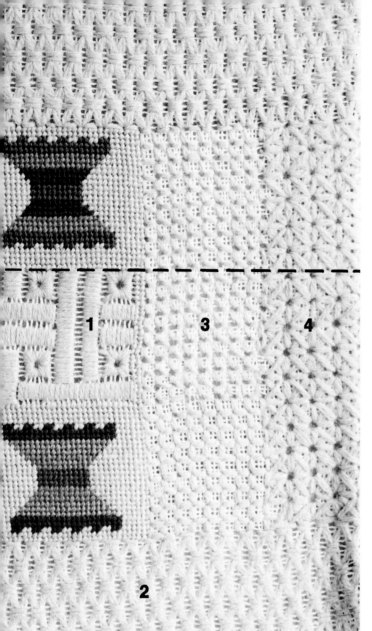

Area below dotted line is shown in the chart opposite.

NATIVE AMERICAN TREASURES

Aleutian Pulled-work Pillow

THE openwork basket weaving done by the Aleutian Islanders resembles Scandinavian pulled work, which is traditionally done with linen or cotton thread on openweave linen. Taking your inspiration from the Aleutian baskets, do this openwork with straw-colored wool on needlepoint canvas, pulling the threads tightly to give the lacy effect of the baskets, adding a touch of color in the central geometric patterns (worked in tent stitch for contrast). Count the rectangles on the graph opposite to mark out the sections for each pattern on your pillow. It is easiest to first divide the canvas in four (as described on page 177) and then count out the pattern from the center, marking the outlines for each block of stitches by drawing a pencil between the threads of the canvas. An arrow on the diagram opposite indicates the center of the pillow. The pulled-work patterns should be done with a blunt tapestry needle threaded with one thread of wool. Pattern #1 is worked with Algerian eyelets over three threads of the canvas, with bands of flat stitch (Gobelin stitch, page 188) in between worked over five threads of the canvas. Pattern #2 is worked in diamond lattice stitch, pattern #3 is faggot stitch, and pattern #4 is Italian cross.

Pull *firmly* to make openwork holes, leaving the canvas partly exposed to become part of the design. You will see that the effect is entirely different if you leave the stitches loose or pull them tightly to form large holes.

If you work on #10 mono canvas (using one thread of Persian wool for the pulled stitches, two for the tent stitches), your finished pillow should measure 13″ x 18″. The whole pillow is shown on page 72, and a detail in color appears on page 70.

ALGERIAN EYELET

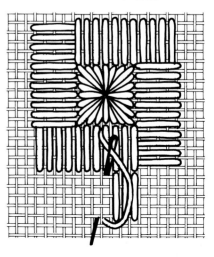

ITALIAN CROSS STITCH

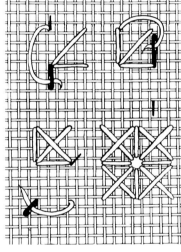

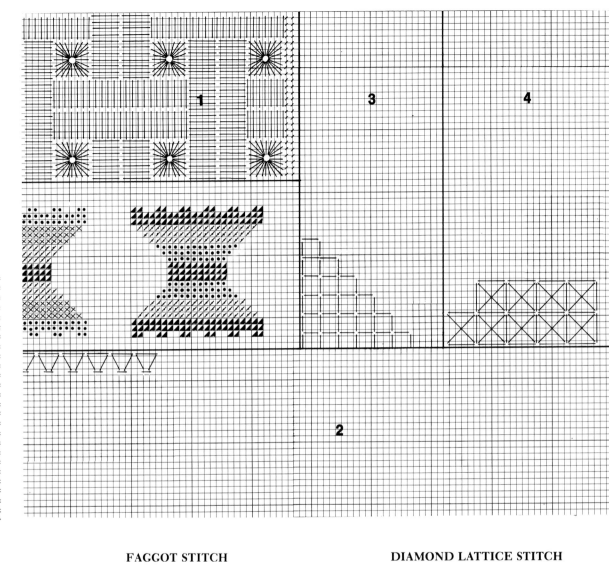

FAGGOT STITCH

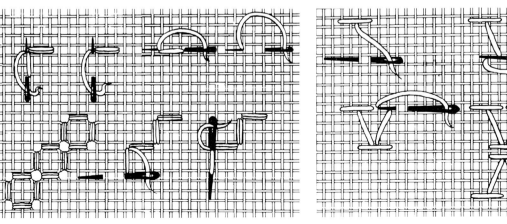

DIAMOND LATTICE STITCH

Rug from Indian Geometrics

FOUR or five stitches were used in this rug and because it's such a simple pattern you could expand it (or reduce it) to almost any size. If you work on #10 canvas (using three threads of Persian wool), you will end up with a rug measuring 23″ x 33″ (or 10″ longer, if you add a fringe at either end).

Outer Border:

1. Working from the outer border toward the center, work one row of slanting Gobelin (slanting three threads up and three threads over to the right) around the outside edge of the design.
2. Work a second row inside, repeating the first exactly.
3. Work a row of cross stitch over two mesh, up two mesh.
4. Work a diamond formed of sixteen cross stitches (over two, up two), as in the graph. There are thirteen diamonds across the bottom and twen-

ty on each side. Note that each diamond shares the cross stitch with the diamond next to it.

5. Fill in the background with slanting Gobelin (over two, up two) lengthwise. Slant stitches in each row alternately to left and right, forming a herringbone pattern.
6. Work one row cross stitch (over two, up two).
7. Work one row slanting Gobelin (over three, up three) all around in the same direction as one.
8. Work one row of cross stitch (over two, up two).

Center Section:

1. Work all diamond patterns in Gobelin stitch in groups of three stitches.
2. Work the center row over four threads and outside rows over three threads.
3. Work square boxes around every other Gobelin diamond, as noted on the graph, in cross stitch.
4. Fill in the background with rows of slanting Gobelin (over three, up three) worked alternately to left and right again, forming a herringbone pattern.

Detail of center section.

COLOR KEY

Tan	1
Gray	2
White	3
Black	4
Indian red	5
Dark brown	6
Burnt orange	7

Inspiration from Baskets

USING simple materials such as jute, string, or even clothesline, some wool, and some needlepoint canvas, you can re-create the effect of Indian coiled baskets and plaques and make a rug, a place mat, a tote bag, or perhaps an unusual wall hanging.

The design opposite was done with natural jute couched in horizontal rows using three strands of brown, white, and rust wool. It measures 17½″ x 24″ and was done on #7 canvas. Count out the pattern, stitching closely over the jute wherever the pattern indicates, leaving the jute exposed in the areas between. The color picture on page 70 shows the finished effect clearly. On the same page is a very strong Navajo design worked in the same way, but using white clothesline instead of jute. You can count this pattern from the black-and-white photo at left. When the couching is complete, cut off the clothesline evenly at either side with a razor blade, or, in the case of a rug, leave it longer to form a fringe. (For couching-stitch instructions, see below.)

COUCHING IN ROWS

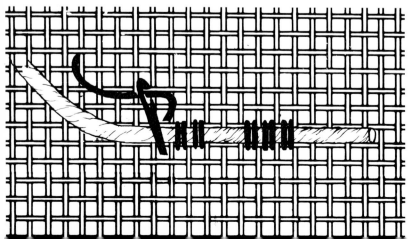

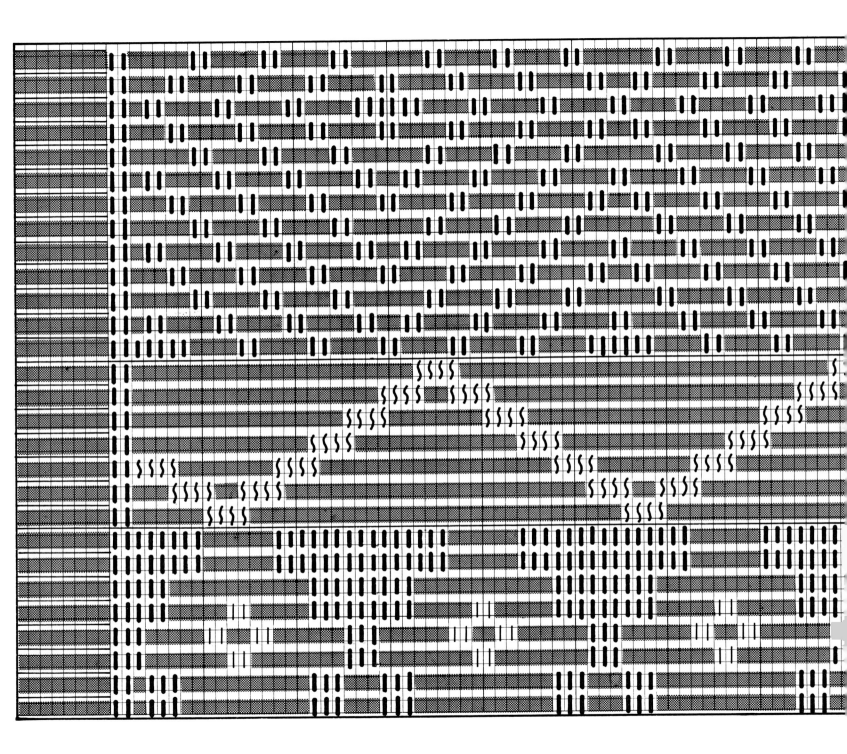

Indian Jewelry

THE design at the upper right, opposite, was inspired by beautiful Indian channel work, where mother-of-pearl, coral, and onyx are set into silver, giving the effect of cloisonné enameled work. I stitched the original necklace on velvet as a pillow, but you could take a single medallion and, working in the same technique, make a piece of embroidered jewelry.

The medallions opposite are intended to fire your imagination to try all kinds of variations on a theme, using the Indian design as a steppingstone to take you into an exciting new world. If we have soft sculpture, why not soft jewelry? You could incorporate the medallions into wide collars with silk braids and cords to link them together, or you could use feathers, beads, padded fabrics, petitpoint, real stones, and silk and metal threads—perhaps even building your jewelry into a garment such as an evening bodice or a vest.

To make the top medallion, cut out postcard pieces slightly smaller than each petal in the diagram shown here and sew each piece down (as shown on page 101). Then cover each with slanting satin stitches, varying the shades of your cotton floss from white to gray, following the dotted lines on the drawing for the direction of the stitches. Then outline with two threads of silver Lurex, couching these down with sewing silk rubbed with beeswax for strength. Work padded satin stitch in the center and for the silver balls between each medallion.

The medallion shown at the bottom has a real turquoise glued into the center and is surrounded by pairs of bullion knots in blue cotton floss, edged between each row with couched silver metal thread. The final silver couching forms a row of loops around the outside. Both jewels may be worked on Ultrasuede or Moccaskin—great material that can be cut away close around the edges without fraying—and backed with the same, with a layer of fusible Pellon (called Stitch Witchery) to hold them firmly together.

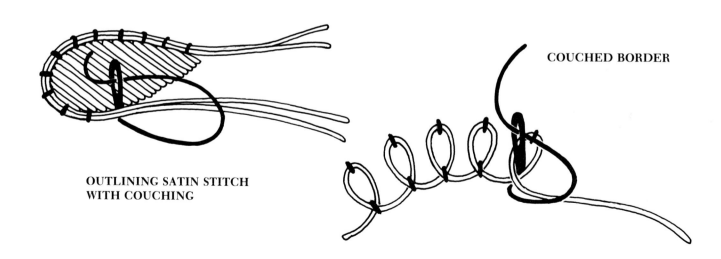

OUTLINING SATIN STITCH WITH COUCHING

COUCHED BORDER

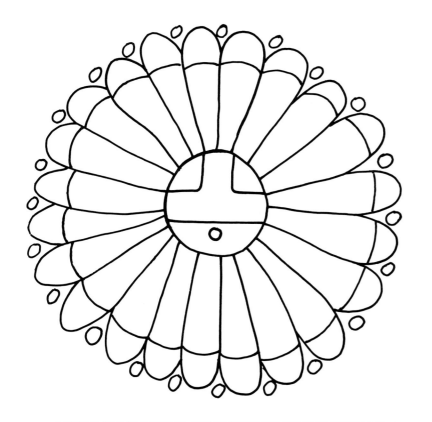

CREATURES GREAT AND SMALL

Table Mat and Centerpiece

WORKING on organdy with simple shadow stitch gives a wonderfully frosty effect, just right for animals in a snowy, moonlit forest.

To make the table mat, enlarge the design opposite to the size you want (the original measured 16″ x 21″) and trace it lightly onto your organdy with a hard pencil. On the reverse side, work shadow stitch as shown below, using three to four strands of white cotton floss in the needle. Begin as shown in the diagram and end off by running the threads into the previous stitches. Since the organdy is transparent, great care must be taken to begin and end off invisibly. Where the areas are too wide for a single band of stitching, work two or three rows side by side, with each row sharing the same holes as the one adjoining it.

To make an unusual floating-candle centerpiece, find a glass cylinder vase and make an organdy shadow-stitched sleeve to fit over it. Transfer the design with half a pine tree at either end, so that when the stitching is complete and both ends are joined you can shadow-stitch the trunk of the tree right over the seam. Slip this sleeve over the cylinder, position the design correctly, and trim the top and bottom, leaving enough turnbacks for a tiny hem at either end. When complete, soak the whole vase in cold water with the sleeve in place and allow it to dry in its own time. This is much more satisfactory than pressing, since you can smooth it flat and pull

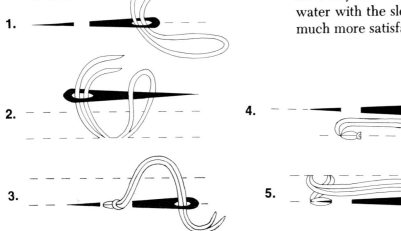

1.

2.

3.

4.

5.

SHADOW STITCH

6.

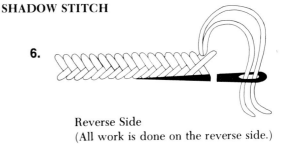

Reverse Side
(All work is done on the reverse side.)

To begin: Cut off approximately a 30-inch length from the skein of cotton floss. Separate two strands, double them over, and thread the four loose ends through the needle. Take the first stitch as shown in the diagram, securing the thread by stitching through the loop. This starts the stitching neatly and invisibly, with no knots. (End off by running the thread back invisibly into the previous stitches.)

7.

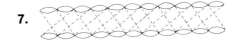

Finished Effect (right side)

it to fit perfectly while it is wet. Half fill the jar with water, float some Crisco oil on top (the whitest in color), and light one of the effective floating candles available in gift shops on top. You can see the effect in color on page 75.

3.

1.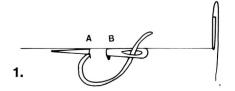

2.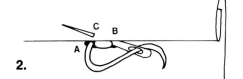

4.

POINT DE PARIS (For hemming table mat)

1. Using a blunt tapestry needle, come up at A under the hem, go in at B and return again at A in the same hole.
2. Go in again at B, and come up at C, directly above A in the hem.
3. Return again to A, and come up at D.
4. Now repeat steps 1, 2, and 3, wrapping each stitch tightly to form large holes.
5. Finished effect.

5.

Peter Rabbit

MY son, Illya, is hugging Peter Rabbit (see color page 79), Beatrix Potter's famous storybook character—who could be anyone's favorite when he's worked in bold needlepoint stitches, with bright blue coat and fluffy turkey work for his tummy and tail. The only trick to making animals in the round is to draw the patterns a great deal wider and fatter than you normally would. When you pad them, you will find they slim down unrecognizably, so if you have drawn them exactly to size they will become disappointingly skinny.

To make Peter, enlarge and trace the pattern opposite on a piece of #6 canvas approximately 20″ x 24″. Using rug wool, you could work the whole animal in tent stitch, but it is much more fun to use textured stitches such as long and short for fur (see below), satin stitch for eyes, split stitch for nose and whiskers (worked on top), brick stitch for the jacket, turkey work for the tummy and tail, slanting satin stitch for Peter's carrot, with fishbone stitch for its leaves, and tent stitch for all four of Peter's paws (including those appearing on the underside). When back and front are stitched, trim the blocked needlepoint, leaving approximately ½″ all around. With right sides facing, sew the front and back together, leaving the bottom open. Turn inside out and cover any canvas showing at the seams by stitching over it with the same color and stitch used at the join. Stuff firmly with Mountain Mist or any suitable padding, hem the base in place, and cover any gaps of unworked canvas here with long and short stitch.

LONG AND SHORT SHADING STITCH

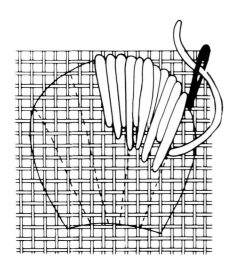 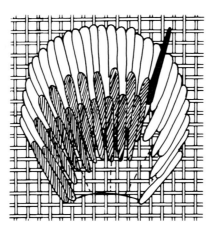 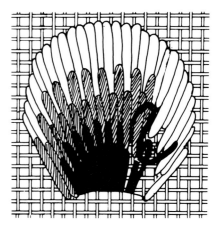

Beatrix Potter's Animals

HERE and on page 79 Cecily Parsley and her rabbit friends done in crewel stitching are contrasted with Peter Rabbit (page 79) in bold latch hooking, and it's interesting to compare the two techniques. The crewel stitching is done with single strands of wool, accented in the shadowed areas with fine back stitching in black cotton floss. Beatrix Potter's illustrations are painted in great detail, with all the atmosphere of old country kitchens—the oak dresser, the china gleaming on the sideboard, chestnuts roasting on the fire—so it's tempting to overpower the animals with their backgrounds. Here is where

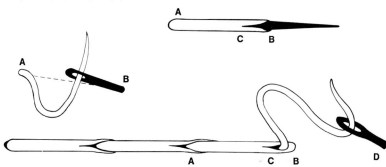

the long split stitch, shown above, is invaluable. By working spaced-out horizontal lines on the flagstone floor in this stitch, you can give the subtle effect of watercolor, suggesting rather than delineating the surroundings.

Peter Rabbit in latch hooking is completely different. The design must be expressive in silhouette, so it must be simplified into blocks of color on graph paper first. Since the design is so simple, you can start at the top and work across row by row, counting out the pattern from the graph shown opposite. This will keep all your wool tufts even and facing the same way. The latch hook technique is explained below, but of course Peter could be equally well worked in needlepoint on rug canvas or in a combination of crewel and needlepoint as is the rug on page 79.

LATCH HOOKING (opposite)

1. Fold the yarn over the shaft of the hook, making sure that the ends of the yarn are even.
2. Hold on to the yarn as you insert the head of the hook under the canvas thread and up into the hole immediately above.
3. Pull the hook back toward you. The latch will open, allowing you to lay the two ends of the yarn between the latch and the hook. Draw the hook toward you and the latch will close around both ends of the yarn. Release the yarn. Continue to pull the latch through the canvas.
4. Give a gentle tug to the ends to secure them.

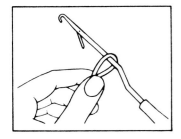

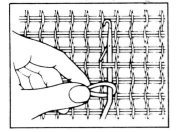

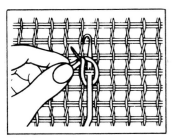

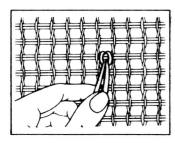

Lion Cubs

THE cubs are worked on #5 canvas in rug wool and are shown in color on page 78. Count them out from the chart opposite, starting with essential details such as the eyes, nose, and then the ears. Once these are in place, you can work all the darkest shadings. This will give you a "skeleton," enabling you to fill in the other colors more easily, using the previously established stitches as check points as you work. Alternatively, you could work across horizontally, counting the stitches row by row, but this is often more difficult when you have to change colors frequently. The background and tree trunk will have great character if you work them in long and short stem stitch, respectively, on the needlepoint canvas (as shown on page 170). Work in dark browns with lighter golden speckles to suggest splashes of sunlight in the dark jungle, but keep all the surrounding colors much darker than the cubs in order to frame them and form a good background.

COLOR KEY

■ Black

◪ Dark brown

◉ Medium antique gold

◈ Light antique gold

⊠ Bright gold

◹ Light gold

⊡ Cream

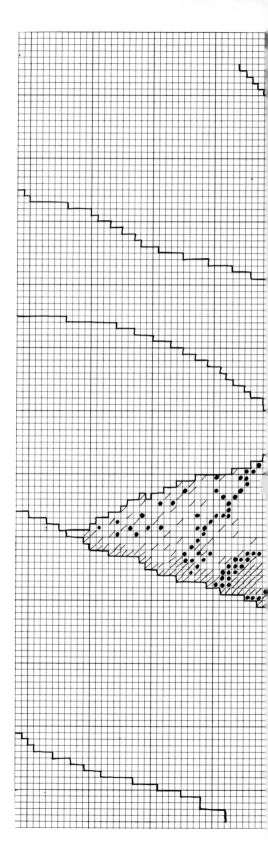

EQUIPMENT AND PROCEDURES

Frames

Most needlework, crewel, needlepoint, and silk embroidery are easier and better worked if the background fabric is stretched taut. Various types of frames and hoops with stands and supports allow you to work with both hands free—one above and one below the frame. In this way you can work smoothly with an even rhythm, just like the professionals. It is essential to have the fabric stretched really tight in order to keep the stitches even.

To mount your work into an embroidery hoop, first remove the outer hoop of the frame. Lay the material over the inner ring with that part of the design that is to be worked exposed in the center. Tighten the screw of the

LEFT TO RIGHT:

Standing floor frame
with 12-inch hoop.

36-inch oval rug frame.

Stretcher strip frame
(available in ½-inch modules).

Lap or "fanny" frame with
10-inch hoop.

(Hoops and bases of the
"fanny" and floor frames
are interchangeable.)

outer hoop (before placing it in position), adjusting it so that it fits firmly all around.

The next step is to pull the fabric taut while simultaneously pressing down on the rim of the frame with your palms. Work around the perimeter in this way until the material is stretched like a drum. Finally, press down the outer hoop. It need not be absolutely flat as long as the material is taut.

Work with your right hand underneath the frame, passing the needle through to the left hand on top. Always keep the same hand underneath the frame and pass the needle vertically through the fabric to the other hand on top. Continue, passing it back and forth vertically in this way, never changing the position of your hands.

To remove the hoop, simply press down on the embroidery with your thumbs, simultaneously lifting off the hoop with your fingers. Do not attempt to alter the screw adjustment before removing it.

Enlarging or Reducing Designs

Enlarging any of the patterns in this book is probably best done by means of a photostat. A photostat service is available in most towns (available through the Yellow Pages under photo copying or blueprint services). One measurement only need be given—height or width—then the designs will be enlarged proportionately.

Another alternative is an opaque projector, available at art-supply or photographic stores. The projector throws a shadow of your design on the wall—larger or smaller according to the distance the design is placed from the projector. It is then possible to tape up your canvas or linen to the wall and trace the enlarged design directly onto it.

Two tips to remember: First, always make sure the projector is lined up absolutely at right angles to the wall. If it is slightly at an angle the image will be distorted; second, once you have begun, don't stop and come back to it later! If the canvas has been moved it will be next to impossible to adjust the image to fit *exactly* over your partly drawn lines.

Transferring

HERE are eleven different methods for transferring designs to fabric. The method you choose is determined by the type of material you will be working on. The chart below shows how to decide on the most suitable technique for your purpose.

Cut your fabric so that the selvages (the woven borders as opposed to the raw edges) run vertically from top to bottom of the design, not across. All woven fabric consists of warp (vertical base threads that parallel the selvages) and woof (horizontal threads woven across). The warp threads are necessarily stronger; therefore, they should run up and down on a picture or a chair seat so that they will take the most strain.

Always work on a square (or rectangular) piece of fabric—cut it to shape after the needlework is finished. Cutting to shape in advance might necessitate cutting lines on the diagonal, which makes the fabric stretchy and easily pulled out of shape. Always allow plenty of extra fabric for mounting and blocking. However expensive, it is cheap compared to your work—and you can always cut away, but can never add so easily!

Always use the same basic procedure when preparing fabric for design transferring. Fold the material in half vertically right down the center and repeat this horizontally. Mark these crease lines by running a hard pencil lightly between the threads of canvas, or by basting lines on fabric. Repeat this on your paper pattern; then, while you lay one on top of the other, align the lines to keep the design centered and square. Edge your fabric with masking tape, or hem, or oversew it all around to prevent fraying while the work is in progress.

FABRICS	Medium-weight linen/cotton	Canvas and eavenweave fabrics	Boldweave textured fabrics, wool and suede cloth	Velvet	Toweling, high-pile fabrics, and knits	Delicate fabrics and blends	Organdy
METHODS							
Back lighting	X			X		X	
Carbon paper	X						
Transfer pencil	X						
Net method	X		X				
Tracing (via tracing paper and see-through fabrics)		X					X
Graphs		X					
Waste canvas	X		X	X	X	X	
Fusible web (Stitch Witchery and Wonder Under)	X		X	X	X		X
Tailor's chalk	X		X				
Basting stitches			X	X	X	X	

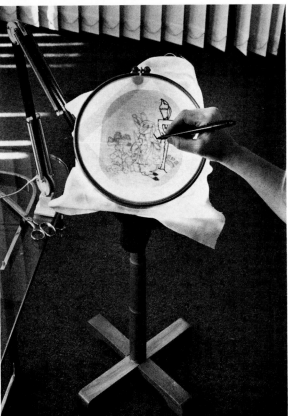

BACK LIGHTING

Stretch your fabric onto an artist's stretcher frame (wooden strips available in art stores). Secure it with tacks or a heavy-duty stapler. Then, with masking tape, hold your boldly traced design to the reverse side, close against the linen. Make sure the edges of the design run parallel to the lines you marked lightly with pencil on the back of the linen to define its borders. Arrange a goose-necked lamp behind the stretcher frame, maneuvering the light so that a clear silhouette of the design shines through the fabric. Trace the pattern with a fine-tipped permanent marker. Did you know that our grandparents used to do basically the same thing—against a window pane? Fortunately, you don't have to be a contortionist when you use this back-lighting method—you can arrånge the light to your convenience, instead of maneuvering to position *yourself* to make the most of the light.

Using a light box is another method of back lighting. This is easily constructed—simply an open box containing an electric light, covered by a sheet of frosted Plexiglas. It helps if the sides of the box are cut down slightly toward the front to provide a slanted surface on which to work. You can then tape the design and fabric square on top of the smooth surface and trace along the lines, which will be clearly illuminated from the back.

CARBON PAPER

Use only dressmaker's carbon (ordinary carbon will smudge). Use blue carbon for light materials, white for dark ones. Establish the center of the fabric by folding it in half and in half again. Crease it firmly to mark the folds, then open up the fabric and hold it down evenly with masking tape on all four sides. A really smooth, hard surface is necessary.

Fold the design into four equal parts, open it up, and lay it down on top, aligning the fold lines of the design and fabric. Now slide a sheet of carbon paper face downward between paper and material. Anchor the paper with some heavy weights—books, paperweights, etc.—and trace around the outline very heavily with a pencil. Using weights is a better idea than taping the design all around, because you can lift a corner occasionally to see how well the carbon is transferring. You really must press down heavily to get good results, and trace with smooth-flowing lines.

TRANSFER PENCIL

This product is available in most needlework stores. Called hectograph transfer pencil, it is available also in specialty stores. It is a speedy method useful for bold designs on washable fabric. Using the pink transferring pencil, outline the design on layout or tracing paper, then turn it face downward and iron it on the fabric, using an iron that is set for "cotton." Do not rub with the iron, since this might move your paper pattern; rather, lift and press —to avoid smudging. The rather broad pink line provided by this method may be washed out when the embroidery is finished.

NET METHOD

Trace or draw your design on paper. Next, lay a piece of net, lawn, tulle, or crinoline over the drawing, and tape it down to prevent it from slipping. With a broad-tipped marking pen, trace your design onto the net. Now lay the net on top of the material and tape it down in the correct position. Once more, outline your design with the broad-tipped permanent pen. You will find that the marker penetrates the net and shows through on your fabric quite clearly. If your background fabric is dark, you may have to just touch it up wherever necessary after you remove the net, to make any faint lines more definite. If your background fabric is light, make sure you test first to see that your felt-tipped marker is not too broad and that your lines do not run through too heavily.

TRACING

Tracing Paper. Tracing is the best method for transferring a design to needlepoint canvas. To begin, draw your design on paper with India ink or with a permanent black felt-tipped pen. Lay it on a table or firm surface and hold it in position with masking tape. If you

used tracing paper, or acetate, place several layers of white paper under the drawing. This will make your black lines more distinct, so that you can see them easily through the canvas.

Establish the center of the canvas and design (as described on page 177). You may find that the center lines on the canvas, although they were marked by the thread, are not entirely straight. This is because the canvas may sometimes be pulled a little out of shape by being stored in a large roll. Just pull the opposite corners and stretch it a little until the center lines are at true right angles again. Then when you lay it on top of your design it will lie flat and your mesh will be square.

Trace the design on the canvas, using a black waterproof felt-tipped pen, or a fine paintbrush and India ink. Test the pen to make sure it will not run when it is made wet for blocking. Then draw the design with a fine light line, because a heavy black line may be hard to cover with light-colored wools. Draw the design as you would on paper, ignoring the mesh of the canvas, and make the lines smooth and flowing. For example, a curve should be a curve and not a series of steps following the square mesh. You will find that you will better interpret a circle with your needle if you draw it smoothly on the canvas, instead of anticipating the stitches with a zigzag drawing that follows the canvas.

If you want to paint your design in color on the canvas, use oil paints. These together with the waterproof marking pens are the best permanent colors to use. Though some acrylics are quite satisfactory, some have been known to run, on occasion. Watercolors will run into your wool when the work is blocked and be hard to eradicate. Oil paint is easy to work with if you mix every color with some turpentine in a small jar and shake well. Then you will have a series of ready-to-use colors that will not be so heavy they clog the canvas or so thin they go pale. Working with them can be just like filling in a children's coloring book, and equally as much fun! Just be patient and allow the paint to dry thoroughly before you start the stitching—up to three days.

Organdy and Similar Transparent Fabrics. Prepare fabric and design as on page 177. Tape the design to a smooth surface, then carefully tape the organdy on top, making sure it is square (it is apt to stretch). Now, using a hard "H" pencil, lightly trace the design. A hard pencil is better to use than pen or brush on delicate fabrics. Keep the lines suitably light so that they will be completely covered by the fine stitching.

GRAPHS

Geometric designs do not have to be applied; they are counted directly from a graph onto the plain canvas or evenweave fabric.

Always begin in the middle and work out to the edges, so that your repeat pattern will be balanced and identical on both sides. Always count the threads of the canvas, never the holes. This makes it much less confusing when you are deciding on the size of each stitch and means your counting will be consistent. One square of the graph represents one stitch on the canvas.

To mark the edges of the design it is not necessary to rule the lines; simply draw the pencil between the threads of the canvas in the same way you marked the center.

To start a geometric design, pick the predominant pattern and work all of this "framework" first. Keep checking by running your needle along the threads of the canvas to make sure that the repeats are lined up correctly. Then if you have made a mistake in the count of this framework you will not have so much to unpick as if you had filled in an entire section. Also, once the framework is made, you do not have to count threads; you can fill in the areas within the pattern by using the outlines as a guide.

WASTE CANVAS

Waste canvas is a thin openweave scrim available by the yard. It is used for transferring geometric designs in cross stitch onto any fabric that does not have a clearly defined weave, such as muslin or organdy.

Baste the waste canvas over the whole area where the pattern is to be. Stretch the whole thing in an embroidery frame and stitch the pattern through both thicknesses, keeping your stitches even by counting the threads of the canvas. When the design is finished, unravel the threads of

the canvas at the edges and draw them right out, one by one. If your fabric is washable, it may be easier to do this if you soak the embroidery in cold water. This softens the sizing in the canvas and loosens the threads enough to allow them to slip out easily.

FUSIBLE WEB (Stitch Witchery and Wonder Under) See page 132.

TAILOR'S CHALK

Available in assorted colors, as a pencils or in blocks, tailor's chalk is excellent for drawing a design freehand on fabric. Start with a simple outline; as you work, it is easy to add more detail. If you make a mistake, the chalk easily rubs out.

BASTING

Buy some batiste, organdy, chiffon, or crinoline, and trace the design onto the transparent material, using a hard pencil. Pin the material with the design to the reverse side. (The inside of a sweater, for instance.) Then baste all around the outlines with small running stitches, using a contrasting color thread. The design will then be transferred onto the right side, and may be embroidered right over the running stitches to cover them. (Or they may be drawn out later.)

Beginning and Ending

WHEN working in a frame, it is easier to keep everything on the surface. Beginning and ending on fabric is best done by taking little back stitches on the right side of the work.

Put a knot in the thread and start on the wrong side of the material. As crewel work should always be backed, the wrong side is not of such tremendous importance, though care should be taken to keep the stitches flat, and

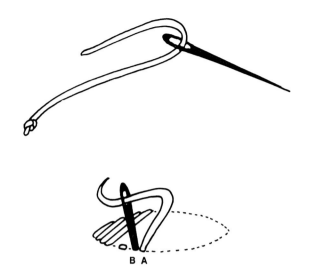

Stretching and Blocking

FINISHED needlework may be pressed or blocked. The latter is preferable, for pressing never brings out the very fine creases in heavy material like twill, or straightens a distorted needlepoint canvas. If, however, you want to press a sweater, for instance, which cannot be blocked, iron it on the wrong side into three or four thicknesses of toweling, using a damp cloth or a steam iron.

The ideal method for blocking all types of finished needlework is with stretcher strips and a heavy-duty staple gun. Artists' stretcher strips (available in art supply stores in all sizes)—wood pieces with mitered corners that fit together to create a frame—are strong, lightweight, and easily stored. They have the advantage of allowing both sides of the work to remain exposed, in case cleaning is necessary. The blocked pieces will also dry quickly since both sides are open.

Begin by buying stretcher strips large enough to fit around the outside of your needlework. Mark the center of each with a pencil. Now fold the square of finished needlework in half and in half again, creasing the folds well to mark the center of each side. Assemble the strips to form a square frame and lay your needlework on top, right side up. Now align the creases on the needlework with the pencil marks on the stretcher strips and staple the four sides, stretching the work out tightly with a pair of pliers. Place staples in the center of each of the four sides, then in the four corners; then work around and around each opposite side until the staples are approximately ¼″ apart.

When the piece is stretched square and tight, run cold water over the needlework (the tub is the best place to work). Wash it gently if it is soiled, then prop it up and let it dry.

B A

not to jump too far from place to place without taking a small stitch in between.

End off with two small back stitches on an outline or inside the shape of a design which will later be covered. (The stitches in the diagram are enlarged to show clearly —they should be very small.) Come up at A and pull through at B, then bring thread to front of work near this position and cut it off.

When working on needlepoint canvas, knot your thread and take the needle down through the canvas six or seven threads away from where you intend to begin stitching, leaving the knot on top. Work toward the knot, covering the long thread on the reverse side. When you have worked up to the knot, cut it off—the end of the thread will be held securely under the canvas by the stitches on top.

When you are finished with a thread, bring it to the top of the canvas some distance from your last stitch. Leave the thread there until, as with the knot, the long thread on the back has been covered by more stitching.

CREWEL STITCHES

HERRINGBONE

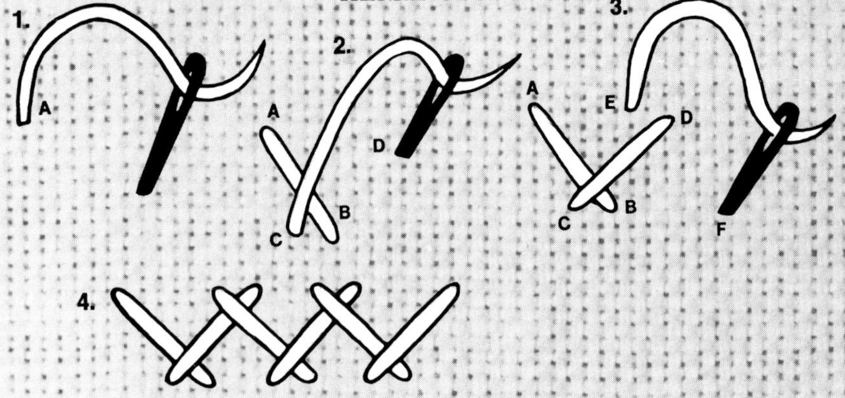

1.
A

2.
A
D
B
C

3.
A
E
D
C
B
F

4.

FISHBONE

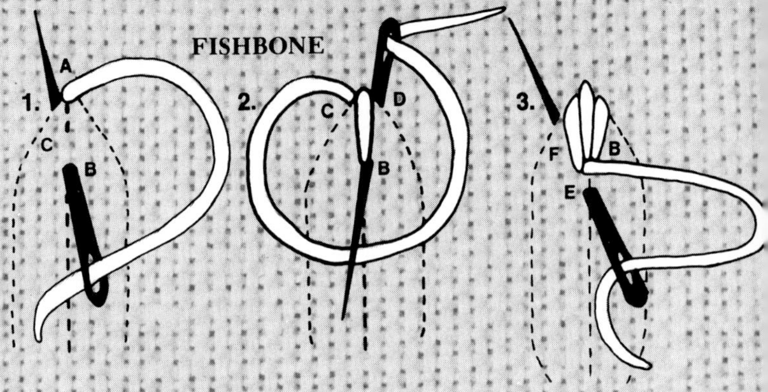

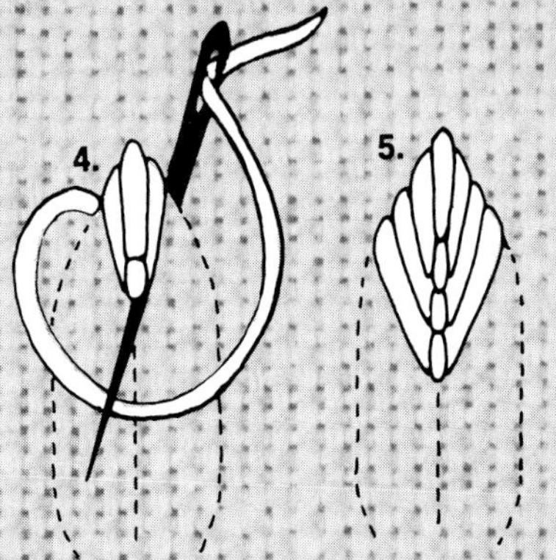

1.
A
C
B

2.
C
D
B

3.
F
B
E

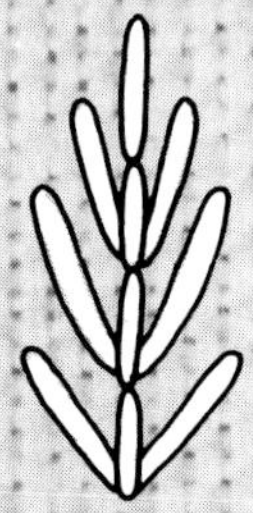

HERRINGBONE, closed

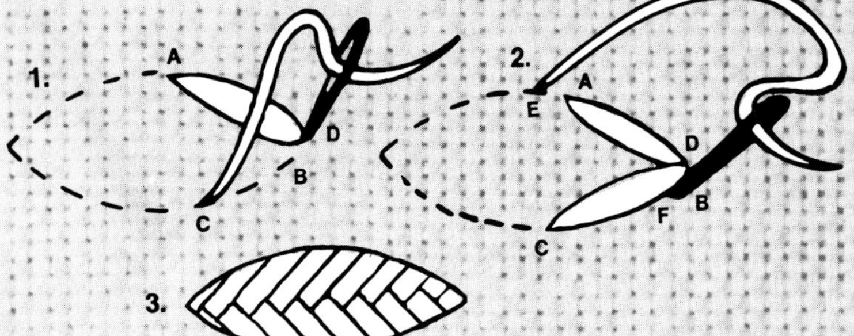

1.
A
D
B
C

2.
E
A
D
F
B
C

3.

FISHBONE, open

4.

5.

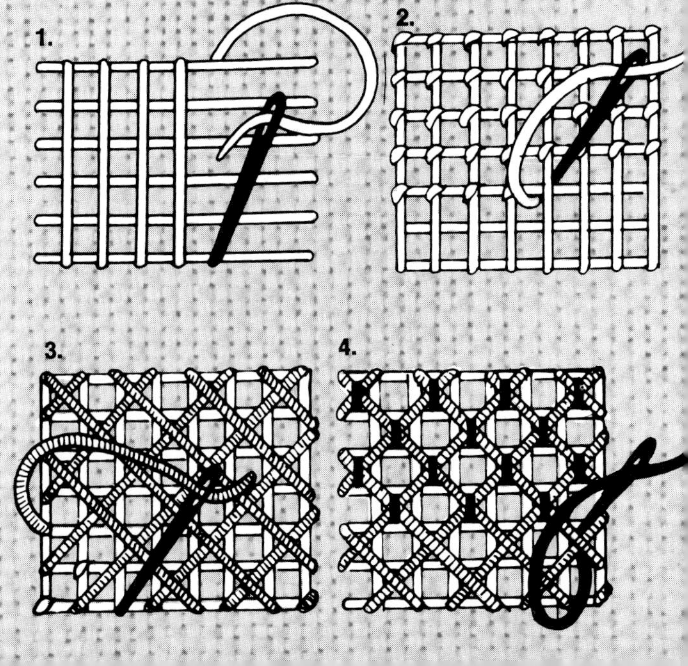

LAID WORK

1.
A
B

2.
A
B
D
C

3.
A
B
D
C

4.
A
B

SQUARED FILLING #1

1.

2.

3.

4.

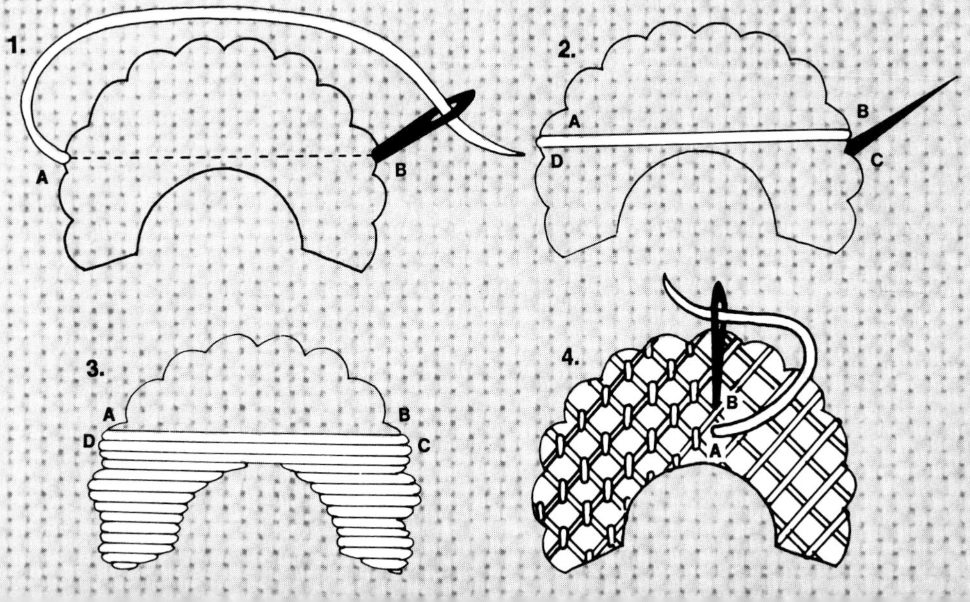

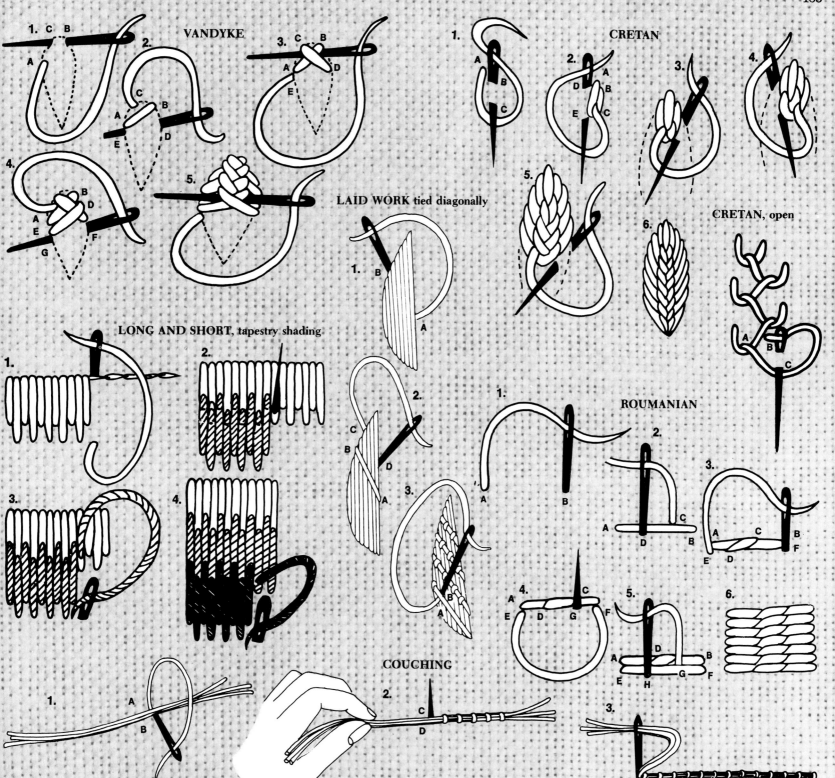

VANDYKE

CRETAN

CRETAN, open

LAID WORK tied diagonally

LONG AND SHORT, tapestry shading

ROUMANIAN

COUCHING

CREWEL STITCHES

CHAIN

CHAIN, open

CHAIN, zigzag

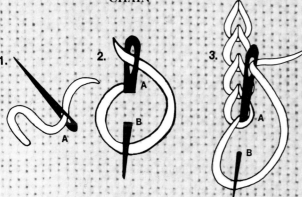

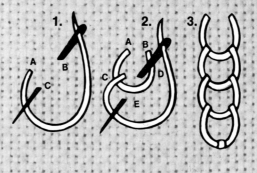

CHAIN, detached (LAZY DAISY)

BUTTONHOLE

ROPE

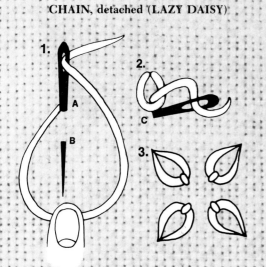

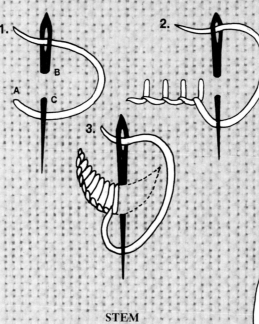

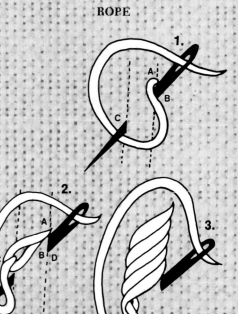

SPLIT

STEM

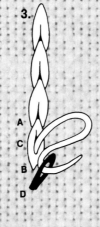

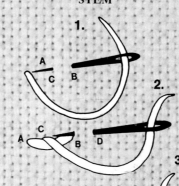

BACK

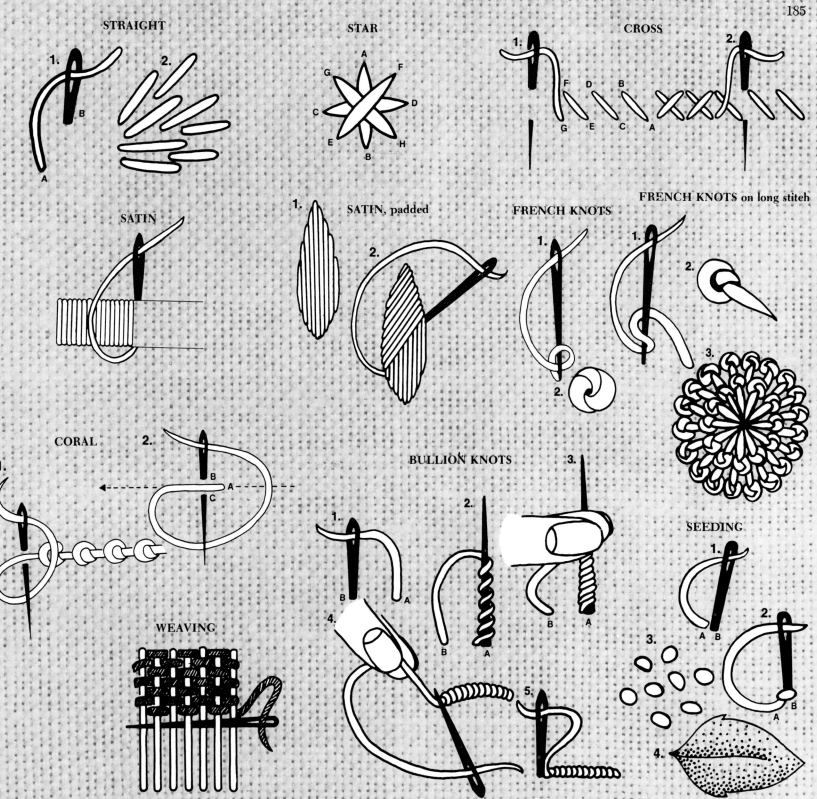

185

STRAIGHT

STAR

CROSS

SATIN

SATIN, padded

FRENCH KNOTS

FRENCH KNOTS on long stitch

CORAL

BULLION KNOTS

SEEDING

WEAVING

CANVAS STITCHES

CROSS, long-armed

TENT, continental

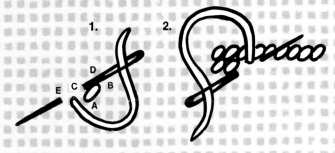

TENT worked diagonally
BASKET WEAVE

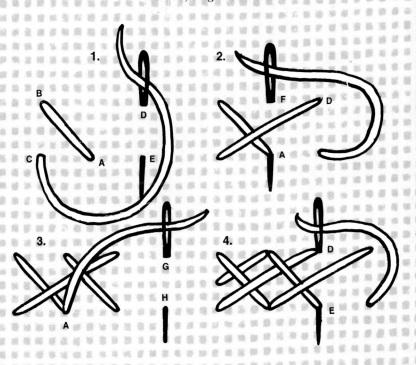

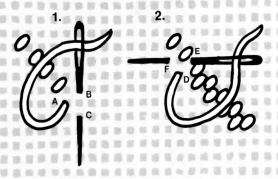

BACK

BUTTONHOLE

TENT, half cross

TENT, reverse

BUTTONHOLE in a circle

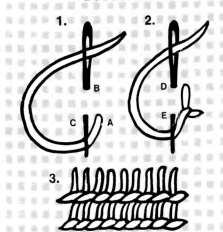

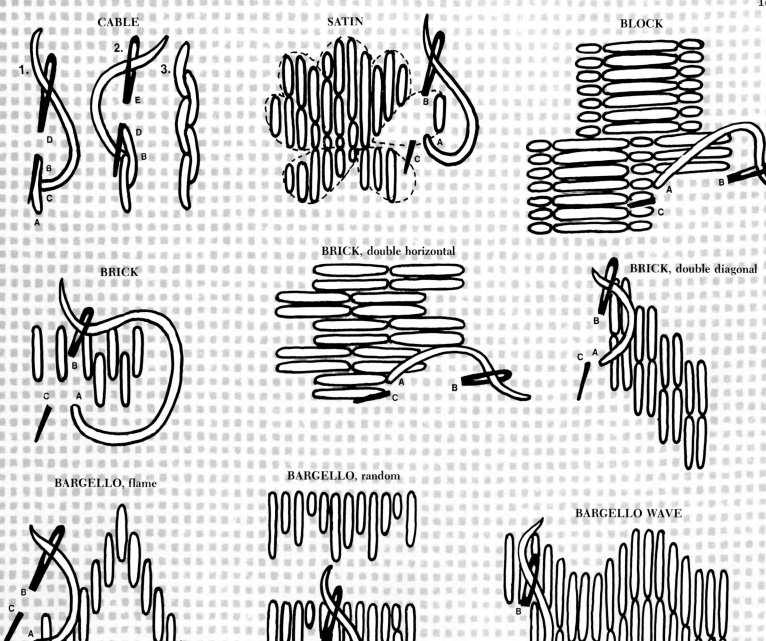

CABLE

SATIN

BLOCK

BRICK

BRICK, double horizontal

BRICK, double diagonal

BARGELLO, flame

BARGELLO, random

BARGELLO WAVE

CANVAS STITCHES

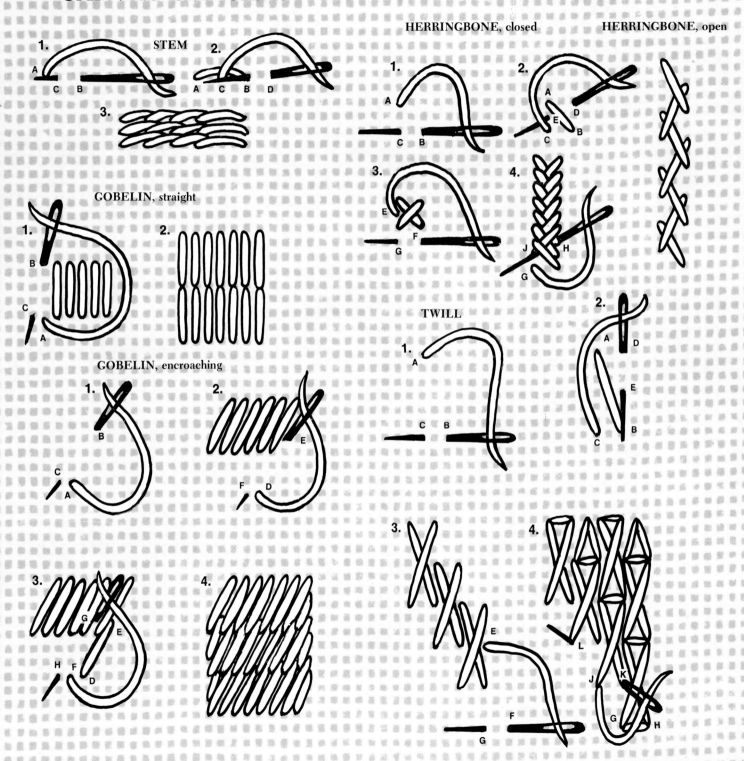

STEM

HERRINGBONE, closed

HERRINGBONE, open

GOBELIN, straight

TWILL

GOBELIN, encroaching

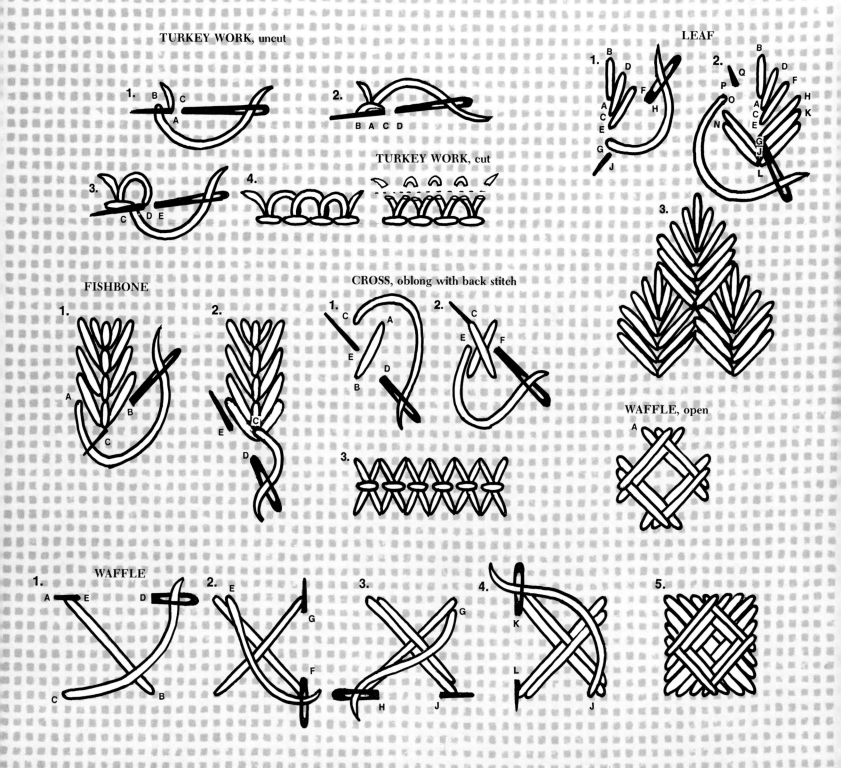

TURKEY WORK, uncut

1.

2.

3.

4.

TURKEY WORK, cut

LEAF

1.

2.

3.

FISHBONE

1.

2.

CROSS, oblong with back stitch

1.

2.

3.

WAFFLE, open

WAFFLE

1.

2.

3.

4.

5.

RAISED STITCHES

CHAIN, raised

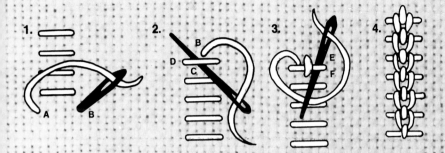

STEM, raised

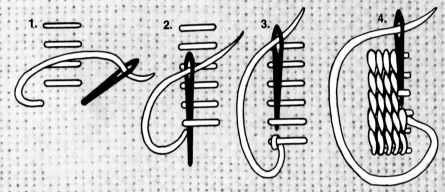

TURKEY WORK

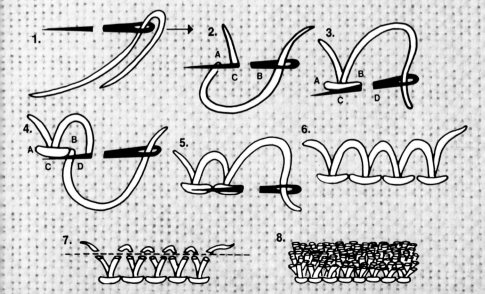

SPIDER'S WEB

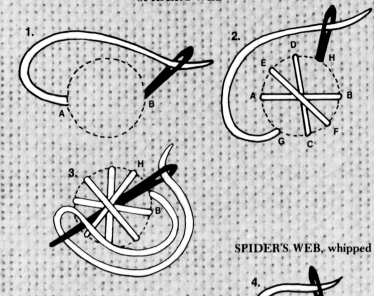

SPIDER'S WEB, whipped

SPIDER'S WEB, woven

SPIDER'S WEB, raised

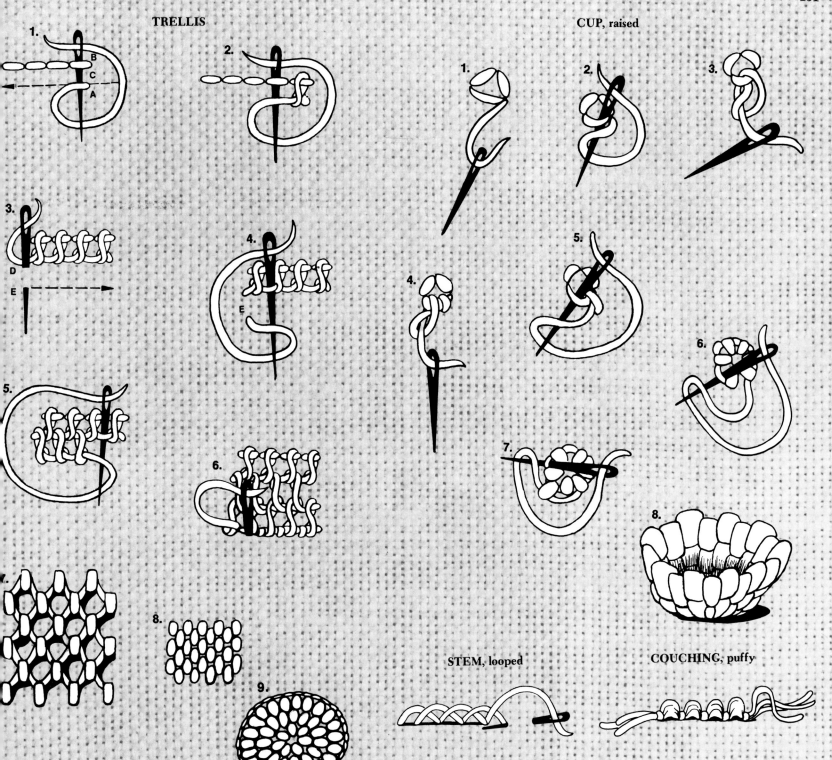

TRELLIS

CUP, raised

STEM, looped

COUCHING, puffy